CIVIL WAR RESEARCH GUIDE

0 11557 02643 6

CIVIL WAR RESEARCH GUIDE

A Guide for Researching Your Civil War Ancestor

Stephen McManus

Donald Thompson

Thomas Churchill

STACKPOLE
BOOKS

Copyright © 2003 by Stackpole Books

Published by
STACKPOLE BOOKS
5067 Ritter Road
Mechanicsburg, PA 17055
www.stackpolebooks.com

Cover design by Wendy A. Reynolds

Printed in the United States of America

10 9 8 7 6 5 4 3 2

FIRST EDITION

Library of Congress Cataloging-in-Publication Data

McManus, Stephen, 1957–
  The Civil War research guide / by Stephen McManus, Thomas Churchill,
Donald Thompson.— 1st ed.
      p. cm.
  Includes bibliographical references (p.).
  ISBN 0-8117-2643-6
  1. United States—History—Civil War, 1861–1865—Registers—Handbooks,
manuals, etc. 2. United States—Genealogy—Handbooks, manuals, etc. 3.
United States—History—Civil War, 1861–1865—Archival
resources—Directories. I. Churchill, Thomas, 1969– II. Thompson,
Donald, 1950– III. Title.
E494.M38 2003
973.7'07'2—dc21

                                                                          2002154372

  ISBN 978-0-8117-2643-6

Contents

Foreword

If we ever tire of our ancestors, we will likely be tired of ourselves. Those who came before us have so much to tell us of how the nation came to be and of how it has kept going. More to the point, the knowledge that an ancestor participated in or experienced a particular event gives that event special meaning to us today. Nowhere is this more evident than with the Civil War, and more Americans are aware of and conversant with the experiences of Civil War ancestors than any other forebears. It helps that by the 1860s we were already a thoroughly bureaucratic people, and the records are abundant despite the loss of much Confederate material in its dying days and the ravages of time and courthouse fires and the like since.

Yet for the first-timer, discovering Civil War ancestors can be a daunting process, as one wonders what there is to find and where to go to find it. Guides for researching Civil War ancestors have appeared in the past, each with its own strengths and weaknesses. But it is time for a new and more comprehensive roadmap, one including the newly emerged electronic services and sources available, as well as the state and local sources too often omitted from older guides. Hence the *Civil War Research Guide*. Whether one is an experienced family researcher or a novice, the sources, their addresses and procedures, and more are all here.

Moreover, this guide gives the hunter a careful assessment of what is likely to be contained in a variety of sources at the national, regional, state, or even county level, as well as newspapers and manuscript collections and even shows and auctions. As well there are useful sample inquiries for those otherwise uncomfortable composing letters, or who are not sure just what they should ask for. Indeed, even professional historians are often not experienced in using some of the sources that are commonplace for genealogists, meaning that this guide will have something to offer to them as well.

Having a distinguished ancestor does not make one a better person (and having a Civil War ancestor who was a deserter does not make one worse, either, though now and then a happy researcher does come upon an unhappy surprise in that line), but knowing your Civil War ancestor does make us better informed and more aware of what our forebears faced and how they faced it. That is all a part of what produces a culture and a national identity, and more than anywhere else, ours was forged in the Civil War by the people whose names and deeds this guide will help to bring to life.

—William C. Davis

Introduction

The purpose of the *Civil War Research Guide* is quite simple: to provide a nuts-and-bolts approach to researching an ancestor who served in the Civil War and his military unit. The guide gives recommendations on how to conduct the research, potential sources of information and materials, ideas on organizing the information you gather, and other useful suggestions.

At the outset, we would like to emphasize that anyone can do this research. At first, we were fairly lost as to how to locate and gather information. The biggest obstacle, though, was to get started. As soon as we sent a few letters, new suggestions and ideas began to pour in. Rather than being "rocket science," this research is an exercise in common sense. The next obstacle was how to organize the materials and information we were receiving. It is our hope that this guide will make things easier for you by letting you take advantage of the trial-and-error approach of our own research.

There are three authors of this guide, who throughout this work are simply referred to collectively as "we." The three of us did not know each other until a couple years ago, and then we met by accident. Each of us had at least one ancestor who served in an obscure infantry regiment, the 18th Massachusetts, which was part of the very well-known V

In 2000, John J. Hennessy of the National Park Service edited and published the memoir and writings of Thomas Mann, who had been a corporal in the 18th Massachusetts from its beginning to end: *Fighting with the Eighteenth Massachusetts: The Civil War Memoir of Thomas H. Mann* (Baton Rouge, LA: Press at LSU, 2000). For us, it was very exciting that this history was published, putting the 18th Massachusetts on the map. Nevertheless, this did not diminish our desire to research and write a comprehensive history of the regiment. As you will find in your own research, the views and motivations of different men in the same regiment are extremely diverse. The story of one person does not begin to tell the story of the regiment, and you will uncover many interesting contradictions as you read through the letters and writings of various soldiers.

Corps in the Army of the Potomac. For whatever reason, a regimental history had never been written on this unit, and, in fact, published materials pertaining to the unit were virtually nonexistent.

We each, individually, had an interest in learning more about our ancestors and their involvement in the war. It quickly became evident that there was very little information available on these individual soldiers. However, an individual soldier is generally part of something larger, in this case a regiment. As a member of this military unit, the individual participated in its operations, shared in its toils and victories, and was involved in the thoughts and discussions of its other members. It dawned on each of us that by researching the regiment, we would be able to gain insight into not only the physical comings and goings of our ancestors, but also their thoughts and motivations, as well as the "community" in which they existed.

After several years of working separately, the research being conducted by Donald and Tom crossed paths. Later, during an eBay auction for the photo of a man from the 18th Massachusetts, Steve's interest in the regiment was discovered. Interestingly, our paths had crossed at earlier times, such as when one of us would visit a local historical society to look at a collection of materials pertaining to the regiment and would learn that someone else had been there before, conducting similar research.

Slowly, a relationship was developed among the three of us, and we joined forces, sharing in all of our work. Our goal was, and is, to gain as much material on the 18th Massachusetts as possible and to write one or more books, preserving the history of the regiment and thereby preserving the history of our ancestors' involvement in the war. Though this may sound

As of spring 2002, when the manuscript for the guide was completed, our collection of materials for the 18th Massachusetts included over forty sets of letters from different men, several diaries and journals, over thirty pictures (and we knew the locations of collections containing at least forty more photographs), pension files for 700 men, and the battle reports and other official military records for the regiment and its men. We had physical descriptions for over 800 of the men, knew the cemeteries where 300 of them were buried, and had identified seventeen sets of brothers who served in the regiment. We also were able to identify several men who were responsible for carrying the colors into battle, as well as some of the drummers; found several misrepresentations as to the men's age at the time of enlistment; and were able to correct errors in the official roster for the regiment.

like a lofty objective, it is quite within reach. Actually, rather than not having enough material for a regimental history, the problem has become that we now have too much information and are faced with having to edit it down to a reasonable level. If you follow the steps outlined in this guide, you too will be in a similar position.

Throughout the book, we generally use the term *regiment* to describe the military unit being researched. Certainly the vast majority of men serving in the Civil War, both North and South, served in regiments, whether of the infantry, artillery, or cavalry. Yet even if your ancestor served in the navy or in some other military capacity not related to a specific military unit, you should still find the suggestions contained in this guide helpful.

In preparing this book, we have tried to compile the most accurate and up-to-date information available regarding names, addresses, telephone numbers, website addresses, and other possible sources. Unfortunately, this information is quite fluid and, particularly with websites, can change quickly and often. Even telephone numbers, particularly area codes, change on a frequent basis.

At some point in time you may find that a website address is no longer valid, an address has changed, or a phone number is wrong. Do not despair. The materials have not disappeared, but finding them will take a little more digging. Call directory assistance or check the Internet, searching the white or yellow pages or using a website such as *www.google.com.*

It is not difficult to conduct the research discussed in this guide, nor is it costly, although it does help if you live in the general area where the regiment was formed. To be successful in your research simply requires an investment of time, some organization, and a desire to learn. This merely involves applying some common sense and a little effort. Good luck.

Chapter 1

Organizing Your Research and Materials

It is important to establish a system for organizing your research efforts and materials. The earlier you do this, the better. Depending on your level of interest and time constraints, however, it is something that can be developed over time. It is likely that your system of organization will evolve as you obtain more and more information and look for better methods to sort and organize the materials.

Your organization system will involve two parts: the physical organization of the papers and materials you collect, and the organization of information and data you extract from the documents. The extent to which you get involved in a system of organization, and the level of detail, will depend upon a number of factors, primarily your level of interest and what you are seeking to accomplish with the research, the amount of information and material you gather, and the number of different sources that you investigate. Spending a little time thinking about the organization of your materials will be very helpful, especially when the amount of information and material begins to grow. The following are suggestions for a fairly detailed system, which you can modify to suit your needs.

PHYSICAL ORGANIZATION OF MATERIALS

Perhaps the best system for organizing the paperwork involved is to place them in manila folders, which are labeled and then organized within boxes or expandable folders. You will need separate folders for the following:

Correspondence

You probably will be generating quite a bit of correspondence. It is a good idea to save a copy of each letter you write, as well as the letters you receive. This way, you will be able to keep track of your requests, to whom you wrote, and when and whether you received a response. This also can be tracked by creating a simple list, either on the computer or on paper. Keep this list updated as you receive responses, and it will provide a quick method for tracking the status of your requests. A blank form that you can use appears in Appendix A.

If you decide to use a paper list, rather than keep it on the computer, staple it to the inside of your correspondence folder to prevent it from being misplaced and make it easy to update as you put letters in the folder.

In addition to writing and receiving letters, you also likely will be making occasional telephone calls, maybe to follow up on some information. When making a call, jot down the person's name, organization, telephone number, and any notes regarding the call. Then put this paper in your correspondence file. This will save time if you later need the person's name and number and will help you remember what you discussed.

Each Individual
Keep a separate folder for each person on whom you have gathered some material. When you obtain copies of letters, pension records, or other information on a new individual, write the person's name, rank, and company on the tab of a folder, place the material in the folder, and then put the folder in the file. Alphabetize the folders on the individual men by last name to make it easier to find the materials on a specific person.

Rosters
Keep a separate folder for the rosters. Even though the roster will be part of a publication with other information on the regiment, put it (or an additional copy) in a separate folder. You will refer to the roster frequently, so it is handy to have a copy of it separate from the other materials.

Materials on the Regiment
Some of the materials you gather will apply to the regiment as a whole. These may be summaries of the regiment's activities, excerpts from books that discuss the regiment's involvement in a certain campaign or battle, references from the *Official Records,* and other more general references. Keep a separate folder for the materials from each source, and label the folder as to the source. For instance, in researching the 18th Massachusetts, some of the separate folders are *Official Records;* references from books on individual battles; Andersonville Prison materials; regimental orders; information on the regiment's uniform; return of the regiment's flags; and photograph collections.

Maps

Another useful folder to have is one for maps. Particularly from the *Official Records* and various books, maps will help explain the activities of the regiment. These maps may not list your regiment specifically, but referring to the brigade, division, or even corps will help you determine where your regiment was located, where it moved, and what part of a battle it was engaged in.

Whenever you come across a map that seems useful, make a copy of it. Along a margin or on the back, write some information that will be helpful, such as the title of the book in which it appeared, the page number, the name and date of the battle or activity being depicted, and any other useful information. Then put it in your map folder.

Others

Create other folders for items that seem useful as you go along. For eample, in the materials for the 18th Massachusetts, one folder contains articles describing an unusual uniform that was awarded to the regiment and another holds materials on the return of the regiment's state flag in the early 1900s. If you think it would be helpful to have some piece or collection of information segregated, place it in an individual folder.

ORGANIZATION OF DATA

It is not necessary to use a computer to organize the data you collect, but it can be very helpful. There are two main types of programs that can be used for organizing your information: a word processing program and a database program.

The uses for a word processing program are probably the most obvious. You can draft letters, create lists, summarize information, and so on. We have transcribed most of the materials we have obtained so that the information can be stored and shared by the three of us.

Another use that may not be so obvious is the creation of a chronology. This is highly recommended. As you gather letters, journals, diaries, and other materi-

> When creating this chronology, there may be parts of the document that you wish to leave out. Use ellipses (. . .) to indicate these omissions so that later you will know where you edited the material by leaving out some of the text. If you add a word or change the spelling, indicate your changes by using square brackets, such as "the rifle misfire[d]" or "the line charged [across] the field." By taking the time to make these notations, you can easily track where you edited the materials, along with the scope of the edit.

als, type the information into a chronology. Use footnotes to identify the source of the information, such as "Jones Diary," or "Smith Letter to Sister dated 3/4/1862, Boston Free Library." Not only will this allow you to follow the activities of the regiment in an organized, chronological manner, but in essence, you will be writing a history of the unit.

In our research with the 18th Massachusetts, we decided to use a database to keep track of the information we uncovered on the men. There are many other uses for a database, and how you choose to use it will be up to you. In our system, we created a separate record for each man, with fields for the following information:

- name
- date and place of birth
- date and battle when wounds were received
- location or description of wounds
- killed in action: date and place
- died of disease: date and place
- promotion: date and rank
- muster: date and place
- POW: when and where held
- transfer: date and to what unit
- discharge: date, place, and reason;
- desertions: date and place
- physical description
- pension record information
- occupation
- death: date and place of burial
- notes: other information of interest

Having this information in a database makes it easy to conduct searches, such as identifying all the men who were killed or wounded in a certain battle or who died at Andersonville Prison. The scope of the database has changed and grown as our research has developed. It is important to have a system that is flexible and allows additions and changes to be made easily.

Date of Birth: [ ] Age When Mustered: [21] Occupation: [Stonecutter]

Comments: [Mustered out 9/2/1864]

Place of Residence: [New Bedford] State: [MA]

Birth Place: [New Bedford] Birth State: [MA]

Height: [ ] Complexion: [ ]

Color of Eyes: [ ] Color of Hair: [ ]

Date of Death: [6/25/1885] Place Where Died: [New Bedford] State Where Died: [MA]

Cemetery Where Buried: [Oak Grove Cemetery] Cemetery Information: [ ]

Town Where Buried: [New Bedford] State Where Buried: [MA]

ID num: [227] Last Name: [Dunham] First Name: [Robert H.]

Regiment: [18th Massachusetts] Company: [A] Rank When Mustered: [Private]

Our database has six pages of potential information for each man in the regiment. This is the first page, which contains mostly general personal information on the soldier. As you see, we are missing some of the information for Robert Dunham, which is not unusual. As we unearth additional information on Private Dunham, it can be easily added to the database.

Date of Commission: [ ]

Date of Enlistment: [9/10/1861] ☐ Drafted Date of Muster: [10/12/1861]

Bounty for Enlisting ☐ Amount of Bounty: [ ]

Date Mustered Out of Service: [9/2/1864] Place Mustered Out: [Readville, MA]

Promotion: [ ] Date of Promotion: [ ]

Promotion 2: [ ] Date of Promotion 2: [ ]

Promotion 3: [ ] Date of Promotion 3: [ ]

Promotion 4: [ ] Date of Promotion 4: [ ]

ID num: [227] Last Name: [Dunham] First Name: [Robert H.]

Regiment: [18th Massachusetts] Company: [A] Rank When Mustered: [Private]

On the second page of the database, we are entering information regarding Private Dunham's general military service record.

Discharge Date: [   ]
Reason for Discharge: [   ]
Place of Discharge: [   ]
Reenlistment Date: [   ]   ☐ Reenlistment Bonus   Amount of Bonus: [   ]
Transfer to: [   ]   Date of Transfer: [   ]
Other Reason: [   ]   Other Date: [   ]
☐ Deserted   Date Deserted: [   ]   Place Deserted: [   ]
☐ Joined Confederate Army
Confederate Regiment: [   ]   Date Joined Confed Army: [   ]

ID num: [227]   Last Name: [Dunham]   First Name: [Robert H.]
Regiment: [18th Massachusetts]   Company: [A]   Rank When Mustered: [Private]

On the third page, we are entering more information about Private Dunham's military record, particularly regarding any reenlistment. We have found a couple of individuals who, after being captured, joined the Confederates, which certainly is quite interesting.

☑ Wounded	☐ Killed in Action Date Killed in Action: [
Date Wounded: [8/30/1862	Place Killed: [
Place Wounded: [2nd Bull Run, VA	
	☐ Prisoner of War Date Taken Prisoner: [
Date Wounded 2: [5/10/1864	Place Taken Prisoner: [
Place Wounded 2: [Spottsylvania, VA	Place Held as Prisoner: [
	Date Released as Prisoner: [
Date Wounded 3: [	☐ Died of Disease Date Died of Disease: [
Place Wounded 3: [	Place Died of Disease: [
☐ Died of Wounds	
Date Died of Wounds: [	☐ Missing in Action Date Missing: [
Place Died of Wounds: [	Place Missing in Action: [

ID num: [227 Last Name: [Dunham	First Name: [Robert H.	
Regiment: [18th Massachusetts Company: [A	Rank When Mustered: [Private	

On this page, we are entering information regarding Private Dunham's medical and casualty history (wounded, killed, captured, missing in action). One thing to keep in mind when entering information into a database is that you need to be consistent with your entries. For instance, here we reference "2nd Bull Run, VA." We need to be consistent in using this abbreviation when entering information on other soldiers, so that we can later do a search for all men wounded or killed during that battle. We strongly suggest that you keep a sheet of paper listing abbreviations, names of battles and other common entries that you are using. Not only will this be a great reference when entering new information into the database but it will assist you in being consistent with your entries, such as using "2nd Bull Run, VA," instead of "Second Bull Run, VA."

ID num: 227   Last Name: Dunham   First Name: Robert H.

Regiment: 18th Massachusetts   Company: A   Rank When Mustered: Private

Additional Information:

Robert H. Dunham: born in New Bedford, the son of Stephen G. and Ruby A. Dunham. He was a 21-year-old stonecutter from New Bedford, when he enlisted on Sept. 10, 1861, and was mustered into the 18th Mass. Infantry on Oct. 12, 1861, as a private in Co. A. He suffered a gunshot wound to the left leg on Aug. 30, 1862, at Second Bull Run and was admitted to Emory General Hospital, Washington, on Sept. 6, 1862, and returned to duty on Oct. 13, 1862. He was wounded for a second time with a gunshot wound to left leg below the knee on May 10, 1864, at Spottsylvania and was admitted to Campbell General Hospital on May 14 from a field hospital. He was furloughed May 18, 1864, returned to the hospital on July 29 and was returned to duty on August 12, 1864. He was mustered out of the army at Readsville, MA, on Sept. 2, 1864. Dunham, who returned to work in New Bedford as a stonecutter, married Mary J. Gifford in New Bedford on Dec. 22, 1867. They were the parents of Alfred S., born Nov. 12, 1868; Ann E.W., born April 13, 1870; and Otis M., born Feb. 26, 1880, all in New Bedford. Dunham applied for an invalid pension on Feb. 17, 1873, and was granted $1.00 per month under Certificate 146111, due to disability caused by a gunshot wound to the left leg. Dunham died, at age 45, at New Bedford on June 25, 1885, due to "Epitheliomia of Testicles." He was interred at Oak Grove Cemetery in New Bedford. His wife, Mary, applied for a widow's pension on Aug. 20, 1890, and received benefits of $8.00 per month, with an additional $2.00 per month for her son Otis under Certificate #: 318314. Mary Dunham died at her home, 309 West Maxfield St., New Bedford, MA, on April 6, 1914.

Excerpt from Declaration for Original Invalid Pension, dated Feb. 15, 1875 (National Archives, Washington, DC, Pension records):
That while in said service in the line of his duty at Bull Run in the State of Virginia on the 29th day of August 1862 he was wounded through the left thigh in action and that at the Wilderness, Va. on or about the 9th day of May 1864, he was wounded in the left leg in action and that he was treated in Emory U.S. General Hospital, Washington, DC and further that he has not been in the military or naval service since the discharge.

Excerpt from Examining Surgeon's Certificate, dated May 5, 1875 (National Archives, Washington, DC, Pension records):
Applicant rec'd flesh wound of upper left thigh, very slight, recovery perfect, no disability also. Ball passed through left, just below bellies of tastrocuerniui (?) muscles. Complains of slight pain after long standing at his work (stone cutting). There is in my opinion, no disability existing, or at least, if any, too slight to be rated.

This page contains the really interesting information regarding Private Dunham. Much of this information comes from his pension records. It is a good practice to make a notation identifying the source of the information, so that you will be able to find it at a later time, when you want to see what additional information and detail you have on that soldier. As you can see, the pension records contain some interesting information regarding Private Dunham's health, both while in the war and after being discharged, as well as some family history.

Invalid Pension Date Filed: 2/17/1873	Inv Application #: 200652
Inv Certificate #: 146111	Initial Pension Amount: $1.00
Widow Pension Date Filed: 8/20/1890	Widow Application #: 338311
Widow Certificate #: 318314	Widow Pension Amount: $8.00
Minor Pension Date Filed:	Minor Application #:
Minor Certificate #:	Minor Pension Amount:
Father Pension Date Filed:	Father Application #:
Father Certificate #:	Father Pension Amount:
Mother Pension Date Filed:	Mother Application #:
Mother Certificate #:	Mother Pension Amount:

☐ Military Record Review   ☑ Pension Record Review

Pension record not found:

ID num: 227   Last Name: Dunham   First Name: Robert H.

Regiment: 18th Massachusetts   Company: A   Rank When Mustered: Private

This is the last page of our database entries, and it focuses on pension applications pertaining to Private Dunham's service in the war.

Chapter 2

Obtaining the Materials

If you think for a second that places will send you original materials from their collections, forget about it. Often you will not even be allowed to *see* the original materials. Why? Because they are fragile and very valuable. Depending on its content, a single letter written by a soldier during the Civil War could be worth hundreds of dollars.

There are wide variations in the nature and type of access you will have to collections of materials. Some places will be happy to photocopy the materials and merely charge you for the cost of copying and mailing. Other places have the materials on microfilm and will lend it through an interlibrary loan program or sell you a copy. Still other places require that you (or someone for you) go to the location and make your own copies using their copy machines. Do not be surprised, however, if some places require you to read the materials in one of their rooms and only allow you to bring in a pencil and paper to transcribe the information of interest.

We have run into all of the above, as well as some other variations. One of us even hired a person who was volunteering at a historical society several hundred miles away, paying him $6.00 an hour plus costs to copy an extensive amount of material. He also did some searches at other historical societies and libraries. This arrangement worked out very well, especially because he already knew how the materials were organized and understood exactly what we were looking for.

If you decide to hire someone to do some research or copying for you, make sure you arrange up front the rate of pay and the maximum amount you want to spend. Take it slow: Start with a small project and work up to a more extensive project after you are comfortable with the arrangement. If you are interested in trying this, ask a reference librarian or historian if he or she can recommend someone you might hire to do the research. Many of them know of volunteers or students who could use the money and who will do a very good job for you.

Overall, you just need to go with the flow. Find out the procedure for obtaining copies of materials from a particular institution, and then figure out how you can achieve it. Do not become discouraged. You may have to delay getting a particular item until some time later. At least you have been able to identify the item and where it is located. You will get it eventually.

Before you visit a place to search for materials, call first and find out their hours, their procedures, and any restrictions they impose. For instance, we knew there was a large collection of letters that we wanted to see at the Boston Pubic Library. In order to see these materials, though, we first needed to obtain letters of reference from libraries or historical societies to vouch for both our reputation and the research we were conducting. These had to be submitted, with a request to view the collection, in advance for approval. When viewing the materials, we were allowed to see only three to five letters at a time, and a person from the manuscript department was present at all times to make sure we did not damage the documents. It took several days to review and transcribe the collection, but it was well worth the effort, and we obtained some fantastic descriptions of the regiment and its activities. With the widespread theft that has been taking place throughout libraries and repositories of historical materials, be happy that such stringent safeguards exist so that the documents you seek do not disappear into the hands of private collectors.

GENERAL POLICIES FOR THE DEPARTMENT
OF RARE BOOKS AND MANUSCRIPTS

Given the fragility of manuscripts, researchers are encouraged to transcribe their contents. Loose manuscripts (except those of the 18th century or earlier), <u>in good condition,</u> can be xeroxed if there is a valid reason, but, in any event only in limited quantities (<u>no more than 20 exposures at one time</u>). Moreover, the requester is expected to return copies after a given period of time.

Due to adverse circumstances presently existing in our library, we are unable to meet any demand for new reproductions of manuscripts other than xerox copies, subject to the limitations specified above. The same applies to rare printed materials. No bound material can be xeroxed.

In order to gain access to our collections, a researcher must register in the reception room of the Rare Books and Manuscripts Department, providing the appropriate identification (a picture ID and, for manuscripts and certain categories of rare books, a graduate student/faculty card or a letter of introduction, on proper letterhead stationery, from a scholar in the field or publisher, addressed to Dr. Laura V. Monti, Keeper of Rare Books and Manuscripts), and a Boston Public Library courtesy card (obtainable at the Book Return Desk, immediately to your left as you enter the Community Library, or at the Book Delivery Desk on the 2nd floor of the Research Library).

Visitors to the reading room can bring only loose paper and pencil.

Readers are encouraged to call or write in advance of their visit, thus enabling the department staff to better serve them.

Our department hours are 9 A.M. to 5 P.M., Monday to Friday, holidays excepted.

The policies for access to the Boston Public Library's manuscript collections. This is very typical of the restrictions that various libraries and larger historical societies impose on people who wish to view the original materials in their collections.

Chapter 3

Identifying the Regiment

Identifying your ancestor's regiment may be the most difficult step in the entire process. If your goal is to learn about a particular ancestor and the military unit in which he served, you will need to know some basic information about your ancestor. It would be ideal if you knew your ancestor's full name and the town in which he enlisted, but even without this information, you should be able to identify both your ancestor and his military unit.

There has been a tremendous effort, by both individuals and government agencies, to document and preserve information and materials related to the Civil War. This includes military rosters, records of service, pension files, military reports, letters, journals, diaries, and other materials. Unfortunately, some gaps do exist. Some records were destroyed, both during and after the war, sometimes by accident, sometimes on purpose, and sometimes by events over which no one had any control, such as fires that destroyed record repositories. While these gaps exist for both the North and South, it clearly is the South that suffers the most from this loss or destruction of records. Even so, this should not create too great of an impediment in identifying your ancestor and the unit to which he was attached.

The Internet is and will continue to be an important resource for Civil War research. The National Park Service is creating a database listing the name and unit of every individual, North and South, who served in the Civil War. When completed, it is expected to contain entries for 5.5 million people. Part of the database is available now, at *www.civilwar.nps.gov/cwss/*, although my efforts to use it have been fairly unsatisfactory. Various individuals and organizations also have websites with rosters varying from single regiments to all of the regiments for a particular state.

Most men, at least initially, were enlisted in regiments raised by the various states and were part of the volunteer army. Almost every state's Adjutant General's Office has published books and reports containing rosters of the men enlisted in the regiments raised by that state. Most of these books

NAME AND RANK.	Age.	Bounty.	Residence or Place credited to.	Date of Muster.	Termination of Service and cause thereof.
Company E—Con.					
Meiggs, William S., 1st Sergt.,	25	–	Abington,	Aug. 24, '61,	Jan. 1, 1864, to re-enlist.
Simmons, Joseph E., 1st Sergt.,	22	–	Duxbury,	24, '61,	Killed Aug. 30, 1862, Bull Run, Va.
Wright, Henry H., 1st Sergt.,	22	$325 00	Plympton,	Jan. 2, '64,	Transferred Oct. 26, 1864, to 32d Inf.
Chandler, Edwin L., Sergt.,	21	–	Duxbury,	Aug. 24, '61,	Oct. 21, 1862, disability.
Churchill, Edmund F., Sergt.,	20	–	Plympton,	July 9, '62,	Sept. 2, 1864, expiration of service.
Dorr, Nathan, Sergt.,	23	–	Duxbury,	Aug. 24, '61,	6, 1863, disability.
Gardner, Leander R., Sergt.,	20	–	Duxbury,	24, '61,	Nov. 4, 1862, disability.
Jones, Henry, Sergt.,	20	–	Duxbury,	24, '61,	Sept. 2, 1864, expiration of service.
Mullen, Martin, Sergt.,	18	–	Duxbury,	24, '61,	Mar. 12, 1863, disability.
Parris, Adna R., Sergt.,	25	–	Duxbury,	24, '61,	Sept 20, 1862, promotion.
Weston, Jabez P., Sergt.,	36	–	Duxbury,	24, '61,	May 3, 1863, disability.
Broadbent, Charles W., Corp.,	20	325 00	Fall River,	Jan. 2, '64,	Killed May 6, 1864, Wilderness, Va.
Churchill, Frederick S., Corp.,	21	–	Plympton,	Aug. 24, '61,	Killed Aug. 30, 1862, Bull Run, Va.
Hodges, Henry W., Corp.,	37	–	Dorchester,	24, '61,	Sept. 3, 1865, expiration of service.
Jordon, John, Corp.,	27	–	Plympton,	24, '61,	Died of w'ds, Oct. 19, '62, Alexan'a, Va.
King, Washington, Corp.,	28	–	Duxbury,	24, '61,	Sept. 2, 1864, expiration of service.
McDonald, Alexander J., Corp.,	27	–	Duxbury,	24, '61,	Nov. 4, 1862, disability.
Ryder, George R., Corp.,	25	–	Duxbury,	24, '61,	3, 1862, disability.
Thomas, Solomon, Corp.,	41	–	Roxbury,	24, '61,	Feb. 27, 1863, disability.
Weston, Henry, Corp.,	29	–	Duxbury,	24, '61,	Sept. 2, 1864, expiration of service.
Alden, Henry,	45	–	Duxbury,	24, '61,	Oct. 30, 1862, disability.
Alden, John,	43	–	Duxbury,	24, '61,	Feb. 21, 1862.
Badger, John M.,	36	–	Oxford,	24, '61,	Dec. 13, 1862, disability.
Bakes, Herbert,	18	–	Duxbury,	24, '61,	Nov. 4, 1862, disability.
Barlow, Edward F.,	20	–	Mattapoisett,	15, '62,	Died Sept. 5, 1864, Andersonville, Ga.
Banes, August,	33	–	Weymouth,	25, '62,	Trans. Oct. 26, '64, to 32d Inf, as abs't sick.
Bishop, Edward,	23	–	Bridgewater,	24, '61,	Died Nov. 10, 1862, Alexandria, Va.
Bonney, Ansel F.,	20	–	Pembroke,	24, '61,	Jan. 1, 1864, to re-enlist.
Bonney, Ansel F.,	22	290 00	Pembroke,	Jan. 2, '64,	Died of wounds, June 30, 1864.
Bonney, Howland S.,	18	–	Duxbury,	Aug. 24, '61,	Sept. 2, 1864, expiration of service.
Bowen, James H.,	30	–	Duxbury,	24, '61,	Dec. 13, 1862, disability.
Bradley, John,	33	–	West Newbury,	24, '63,	Transferred May 3, 1864, to Navy.
Brabrook, William F.,	18	–	Chelsea,	24, '61,	June 16, 1862, disability.
Broadbent, Charles W.,	18	–	Fall River,	24, '61,	Jan. 1, 1864, to re-enlist.
Brown, Edwin,	23	–	Candia, N. H.,	24, '61,	Sept. 2, 1864, expiration of service.
Bryant, George,	32	–	Duxbury,	July 17, '63,	Transf. Oct. 26, '64, to 32d Inf, pris'r war.
Bryden, Robert B.,	24	–	Boston,	Aug. 24, '61,	Feb. 22, 1862, disability.
Burgess, Jacob S.,	29	–	Duxbury,	24, '61,	Sept. 2, 1864, expiration of service.
Butler, John S.,	22	–	Duxbury,	24, '61,	Oct. 11, 1862, disability.
Caswell, Orin E.,	21	–	Middleborough,	July 4, '62,	Jan. 1, 1864, to re-enlist.
Caswell, Orin E.,	23	325 00	Middleborough,	Jan. 2, '64,	Trans. Oct. 26, '64, 32d Inf, abs. with't l've.
Chandler, Herbert A.,	18	–	Duxbury,	Aug. 24, '61,	Feb. 22, 1862, disability.
Church, David F.,	18	–	Duxbury,	24, '61,	Killed Aug. 30, 1862, Bull Run, Va.
Churchill, Josiah F.,	20	–	Plympton,	July 9, '62,	Dec. 13, 1862, disability.
Clark, Freeman,	37	–	Mattapoisett,	Aug. 12, '62,	28, 1863, disability.
Clark, Hiram A.,	22	–	Plympton,	July 9, '62,	Jan. 11, 1863.
Connelly, William F.,	24	–	Weymouth,	Aug. 26, '63,	Deserted Oct. 16, 1863.
Cook, John A.,	17	–	Abington,	24, '61,	
Cox, Charles I.,	38	–	Duxbury,	24, '61,	Jan. 9, 1863.
Cox, Hiram G.,	31	–	Duxbury,	24, '61,	Feb. 8, 1864, to re-enlist.
Cox, Hiram G.,	33	384 66	Duxbury,	Feb. 9, '64,	Transferred Oct. 26, 1864, to 32d Inf.
Covert, Eugene S.,	23	–	Mattapoisett,	Aug. 6, '62,	Sept. 2, 1864, expiration of service.
Davidson, George H.,	22	–	Duxbury,	24, '61,	May 8, 1864, do do
Delano, Otis,	18	–	Duxbury,	24, '61,	Sept. 28, 1862, disability.
Dowd, James J.,	20	–	Quincy,	24, '61,	2, 1864, expiration of service.
Drake, Charles F.,	24	–	Pembroke,	24, '61,	2, 1864, do do
Dunham, William H.,	27	–	Biddleborough,	19, '62,	2, 1864, do do
Elliott, John,	24	–	Bridgewater,	24, '61,	Jan. 1, 1863, disability.
Gallon, James,	42	–	Mattapoisett,	15, '62,	Transferred May 1, 1864, to V. R. C.
Glover, John,	38	–	Duxbury,	24, '61,	Jan. 24, 1862, disability.
Graves, Francis G.,	21	–	Marlborough,	24, '61,	Died Aug. 30, 1862, Belle Isle, Va.
Harris, Lebbeus,	38	–	Duxbury,	24, '61,	Dec. 24, 1861, disability.
Hayden, Oliver,	31	–	Stoughton,	24, '61,	9, 1861, disability.
Holbrook, Ara W.,	27	–	Braintree,	24, '61,	Jan. 1, 1864, to re-enlist.
Holbrook, Ara W.,	29	325 00	Stoughton,	Jan. 2, '64,	Transferred Oct. 26, 1864, to 32d Inf.
Joyce, Edward,	30	–	Kingston,	Aug. 24, '61,	Jan. 21, 1862, disability.
Keith, Howard,	42	–	No. Bridgewater,	24, '61,	Transferred to V. R. C., no date.
Kimball, Samuel,	41	–	No. Bridgewater,	24, '61,	Killed Aug. 30, 1862, Bull Run, Va.
Lapham, Constant C.,	18	–	Duxbury,	24, '61,	Jan. 16, 1863, disability.
Leavitt, Jarius W.,	25	–	Duxbury,	24, '61,	Dec. 19, 1862, disability.
Loner, William E.,	25	–	Lakeville,	16, '62,	Transferred to V. R. C.
Luce, Franklin W.,	24	–	Tisbury,	24, '61,	Jan. 7, 1862, disability.
Magoun, Edward M.,	22	–	Duxbury,	24, '61,	Sept. 2, 1864, expiration of service.
Marshall, William L.,	24	–	Taunton,	24, '61,	Transferred to V. R. C.
Mears, Samuel G.,	24	–	Hingham,	24, '61,	Mar. 16, 1865, expiration of service.
Meechan, David C.,	23	–	Duxbury,	24, '61,	Transferred Oct. 26, 1864, to 32d Inf.
Meiggs, William S.,	27	325 00	Abington,	Jan. 1, '64,	Transferred Oct. 26, 1864, to 32d Inf.
McCarty, John,	39	50 00	Boston,	July 20, '63,	Transferred Oct. 26, 1864, to 32d Inf.
McDonald, Richard,	34	–	Marshfield,	Aug. 26, '63,	Deserted Oct. 16, 1863.

Adjutant-General, *Record of Massachusetts Volunteers: 1861–1865*, vol. II, (Boston: Wright & Potter, 1870), p. 288. The format of this roster includes a brief statement regarding the date and cause for each soldier's termination of service, along with some brief information as to the men's age, residence, and date of enlistment.

COMPANY "D"

Alden, Leander M. — Priv. — Res. Middleboro; 31; shoe cutter; enl. May 14, 1861; must. Aug. 24, 1861; must. out Sept. 2, 1864.

Alden, Marcus M. — Priv. — Res. Middleboro; 18; shoemaker; enl. May 10, 1861; must. Aug. 24, 1861; re-enlist. Jany. 1, 1864; transf. Oct. 21, 1864, to 32d Mass. Inf. See Co. "A" 32d Mass. Inf.

Atwood, Daniel W. — Priv. — Res. Middleboro; 26; clerk; enl. June 10, 1861; must. Aug. 24, 1861; disch. for disability, Nov. 12, 1862, Boston, Mass. See V. R. C.

Baker, John S. — Priv. — Res. Middleboro; 38; saloon keeper; enl. June 21, 1861; must. Aug. 24, 1861; disch. Oct. 20, 1861, at Hall's Hill, Va.

Barry, Michael — Priv. — Res. Roxbury; 36; laborer; enl. and must. Dec 29, 1862; wounded June 3, 1864, at Bethesda Church, Va.; transf. Oct. 21, 1864, to 32d Mass. Inf. See Co. "A" 32d Mass. Inf.

Belas, Solomon F. — Sergt. — Res. Middleboro; 31; shoemaker; enl. April 27, 1861; must. Aug. 24, 1861; re-enlist. Feb 7, 1864; wounded in 1864; must. out Nov. 2, 1864.

Benson, Peleg F. — Priv. — Res. Middleboro; 27; shoemaker; enl. May 16, 1861; must. Aug. 24, 1861; died Nov. 17, 1862, of disease, at Washington, D.C.

Benson, William — Priv. — Res. Middleboro; 23; peddler; enl. May 10, 1861; must. Aug. 24, 1861; disch. Nov. 24, 1862.

Bodge, Samuel D. — Priv. — Res. Boston; 28; painter; draft and must. Aug. 25, 1863; missing May 5, 1864, Wilderness, Va.; died Aug. 1, 1864, at Andersonville, Ga., a Prisoner of War.

Briggs, Jesse H. — Priv. — Res. South Bridgewater; 21; shoemaker; enl. Aug. 19, 1861; must. Aug. 24, 1861; wounded Dec. 13, 1862, Fredericksburg, Va.; disch. for disability, Jany. 5, 1864.

Brightman, William R. — Priv. — Res. Middleboro; 22; tailor; enl. May 10, 1861; must. Aug. 24, 1861; died of disease, Nov. 20, 1862, at Richmond, Va.

Brown, Charles I. — Priv. — Res. Middleboro; 25; shoemaker; enl. May 14, 1861; must. Aug. 24, 1861; wounded May 3, 1863, Chancellorsville, Va., as Corpl.; re-enlist. Feb 7, 1864; transf. Oct. 21, 1864, to 32d Mass Inf. See Co. "D" 32d Mass. Inf.

Burbank, Charles M. — Priv. — Res. Mattapoisett; 22; ship carpenter; enl. June 18, 1861; must. Aug. 24, 1861; disch. Jany. 16, 1863, Washington, D.C.

Thomas Wentworth Higginson, *Massachusetts in the Army and Navy: During the War of 1861–65* **(Boston: Wright & Potter Printing Co., 1895), p. 369. This version of the roster includes the soldier's occupation prior to enlistment.**

include an index listing all of the men alphabetically, along with the unit or units they served in (because of promotions and reenlistments, some men served in more than one unit during the war). Appendix D lists the books that were published by the various states—some states have more than one set of books that can be searched—as well as websites with full or partial rosters.

If you do not know the state where your ancestor enlisted, you may still be able to locate him through the pension records database, discussed in the chapter on the National Archives. Although the National Archives contain pension records only for men serving the Union, the individual states making up the Confederacy issued pensions to their men, and various sources for this information are listed in Appendix J.

The materials may list several men with the same or similar names, and there may be several different spellings for the same name in various records, rosters, and books. These materials have been known to contain typos, so you may need to look for names similar to that of your ancestor. Research on a German immigrant with the last name of Isselmann turned up four different spellings. What can make it even more difficult is that occasionally the men themselves used different spellings for their names, such as Francis Nunes, who also went by Noons.

Having identified one or more listings in the index, start turning to the pages indicated. Generally the index will refer you to a page or pages in the associated volumes where the man's name appears. Often this will be the page of a roster for an individual regiment. In the roster, you may find such information as the town where the man enlisted, the company to which he was assigned, the date of enlistment, rank, dates of any promotions, his profession, and perhaps dates on which he was wounded or killed, was taken prisoner, deserted, or was discharged. There may be other information as well.

Often it will be easy to locate an ancestor, but others require the process of elimination. You may need to compare the roster information on several people to determine which one is your ancestor. This should be an exercise in common sense, such as whether the town where he enlisted is in the area where he lived; the age is approximately correct; or the rank and service agree with what you know from family stories about his history. Clearly, the more you know about the person, the easier this is.

If you still cannot identify the person, you need to do some genealogy research—create a family tree and keep working backward. The best source for information is your family. Together, you should be able to put together a surprisingly comprehensive family tree. Other sources can be found at the local public library and town hall where your family is from, or possibly through one of the commercially available "family tree" type of computer programs or websites.

Once you have found the person you are interested in from the index and then traced him to a roster for an individual regiment, you have gained a wealth of information. In addition to the information contained in the roster, which can be fairly extensive, there will be a brief summary of the activities of that regiment. These summaries typically were prepared for each year of the regiment's service. Although fairly brief and usually very dry in their descriptions, they give a brief overview of the regiment, what it did year by year, the battles it was involved in, how it fit into the larger structure of the army, and a list of the men in the unit.

Many states have more than one set of reports, often using different sources, that summarize the activities of the regiments raised by that state. Check each source, as two different series of reports often contain different details regarding the information listed for each man in the roster. This difference probably is attributable to the authors using different sources for their information, or it could be that they were only interested in reporting information they felt was relevant to their particular task.

The Internet should not be overlooked as a source of information on the regiment. Some of the information you find may be of a very general nature, but in some cases you will be amazed at the detail that is presented.

Chapter 4

Chronology
and Army Structure

Throughout your research, it will be extremely helpful to have a chronology of the battles in which the regiment was involved and a chart showing how it fits within the overall military picture. These items will be useful for turning up possible sources of information, such as materials located at national battlefield parks, and identifying other units that fought alongside your regiment.

CHRONOLOGY OF BATTLES AND ENGAGEMENTS
Creating a chronology of the battles and engagements involving your regiment is very easy. Appendix E has a form you can use, with one column for the dates of the battles and a second for the names of the battles. Do not expect to fill out this form all at once, but add to it as you gather information. If you already have located the brief histories from the reports published by the state, then you are well on your way to listing many of the battles, particularly the major engagements, in which the regiment participated.

CHARTS OF ARMY AND REGIMENTAL STRUCTURE
Both the North and South followed the same basic military structure and hierarchy for their armies and navies. This is not surprising, as the leaders of both sides had undergone the same military training and learned the same military strategies and tactics, and in fact, many had served together in the military prior to the outbreak of the Civil War.

We have been discussing the regiment as a single military unit. Yet a regiment had substructures that should be noted as part of your research. A regiment was grouped with several other regiments to create a brigade. Several brigades were grouped together to form a division, and several divisions were grouped together to form a corps. And finally, several corps were combined to form an army. Both the North and South had several different armies. A chart depicting this general structure would be something like the following:

ARMY OF THE POTOMAC

—I Corps
—II Corps
—III Corps
—V Corps

    —1st Division
        —1st Brigade
            —1st Michigan
            —18th Massachusetts
            —25th New York
            —118th Pennsylvania
        —2nd Brigade
        —3rd Brigade

    —2nd Division
        —1st Brigade
        —2nd Brigade
        —3rd Brigade

While researching your regiment, it helps to understand how a regiment is formed and the details of its structure. Particularly during the first couple years of the war, both the North and South raised regiments of volunteers. This was accomplished through various means and often it resulted in towns and cities making efforts to enlist men for the war effort. When a town had raised a group of men, they were grouped together and then sent to an enlistment or training camp. The men also were credited as having been raised by that specific town. Typically these men were placed in groups of 100 to form a company, and most of the men in a specific company were from a specific town or region.

Usually at the training camp, the state would decree that a regiment should be formed, and ten companies were combined and designated as a regiment. Often these companies had been raised from the same general geographic region. Each regiment was assigned a unique identifying number, and each company was designated by a unique letter. The regiment was then inducted into the service of the government.

The head officer of a regiment was a colonel. As part of his staff was a lieutenant colonel and then a major. The regimental staff also contained other members, both officers and noncommissioned officers. Each company was headed by a captain, who had under him various first and second lieutenants, sergeants, corporals, and approximately eighty privates.

It is very useful to create a chart depicting the initial formation of your regiment, identifying the colonel, the main officers for each of the companies, and the town from which each company originated. From this, you can identify local libraries, historical societies, and newspapers to contact for potential records and materials. Also, as the colonel or head of the regiment prepared the regiment's official military reports, knowing this person's name will assist in finding references to the regiment, both in the official military records and in books describing battles and campaigns.

The person in charge of the regiment was often subject to change, due to promotion, death, injury, sickness, and so on. You can expect at least a dozen different people to have led a regiment during the war. Sometimes the rank of the person in charge was as low as that of the senior captain, and during a particularly difficult battle, the regiment may have been led by someone of an even lower rank. It is useful to track the identity of the person in charge, especially at the time of battles and engagements involving the regiment.

The following is a chart for the 18th Massachusetts at the time of its formation. Appendix F has a chart you can use to fill in the information pertaining to your regiment.

18TH MASSACHUSETTS VOLUNTEER INFANTRY, COL. JAMES BARNES

Company	Captain	Town of Origin
A	Lewis Tucker	Boston
B	George C. Ruby	Taunton
C	William McFarlain	Carver
D	Stephen Thomas	Middleborough

18TH MASSACHUSETTS VOLUNTEER INFANTRY, COL. JAMES BARNES *(continued)*

Company	Captain	Town of Origin
E	Thomas Weston	Duxbury
F	Henry Onion	Dedham
G	William B. White	Hanover
H	Joseph Collingwood	Plymouth
I	Frederick D. Forest	Wrentham
K	John L. Spaulding	Quincy

The next useful step is to track where your regiment falls within the overall army organization. Because a brigade generally acted together, the activities of one regiment usually were the same as those of all the other regiments in that brigade. If the information you are able to locate pertaining directly to your regiment is scarce, looking at information available for other regiments in the same brigade will allow you to track, at least indirectly, the activities of your regiment.

In addition to the regiment you are researching, it is also helpful to identify who was in charge of the other regiments in the same brigade, as well as who was in charge of the brigade, the division, and the corps. Many of the books being written on Civil War battles and campaigns are very detailed and contain copious footnotes identifying the sources used. Often the index lists the pages where specific regiments and people are mentioned in the book. By knowing the names of the regimental commanders and those in charge of the brigade, division, and corps, as well as other regiments in the brigade, you can look through the index for references to these individuals and regiments. It is possible that although your particular regiment and commander are not identified, another regiment in the same brigade may have several references and citations. Looking at the portions of the book describing the actions of the other regiments, and of the brigade as a whole, will give you a good idea as to what your ancestor and his regiment were doing during the battle.

Where your regiment fits within the command structure of the army will have had many changes over time. It was not unusual for regiments to be moved from one brigade to another, as requirements dictated. These changes in the command structure are usually well documented and easy to find. If changes were made, they usually went into effect in the spring and fall, which corresponded to either the beginning of the spring campaign or the end of campaigning for the year. One source that is excellent for tracking these changes is the *Official Records,* discussed in Chapter 11 on Books.

The following is a sample outline of the command structure involving the 18th Massachusetts. Appendix G contains one that you can copy and fill in as you obtain this information for your own regiment.

June 1863

V Corps	Maj. Gen. George Sykes
1st Division	Brig. Gen. James Barnes
1st Brigade	Col. William Tilton
18th Massachusetts	Col. Joseph Hayes
22nd Massachusetts	Lt. Col. Tom Sherwin, Jr.
1st Michigan	Col. Ira C. Abbott
118th Pennsylvania	Lt. Col. James Gwyn

October 1863

V Corps	Maj. Gen. George Sykes
1st Division	Brig. Gen. Charles Griffin
1st Brigade	Brig. Gen. James Barnes
18th Massachusetts	Col. William White
22nd Massachusetts	Col. William Tilton
1st Michigan	Lt. Col. William Throop
118th Pennsylvania	Maj. Charles Herring

Having charts of the command structure from the beginning of your regiment's enlistment through the time it was mustered out of service can be extremely valuable. It will help ensure that you do not overlook important sources of information, particularly if it is difficult to locate sources directly pertaining to your regiment. It also provides an easy checklist of regiments and people's names to look for when reading books about different battles or scanning their indexes.

This outline of the command structure also can help you pinpoint your regiment on maps detailing the locations of divisions, brigades, and regiments. Some excellent map studies have been published on the major battles, and even with some of the less detailed maps, it may be possible to identify the location of your regiment with a reasonable degree of certainty.

ARTILLERY BRIGADE.

Col. JOHN C. TIDBALL.

Maine Light, 6th Battery (F), Capt. Edwin B. Dow.
Massachusetts Light, 10th Battery, Capt. J. Henry Sleeper.
New Hampshire Light, 1st Battery, Capt. Frederick M. Edgell.
1st New York Light, Battery G, Capt. Nelson Ames.
4th New York Heavy, 3d Battalion, Lieut. Col. Thomas Allcock.
1st Pennsylvania Light, Battery F, Capt. R. Bruce Ricketts.
1st Rhode Island Light, Battery A, Capt. William A. Arnold.
1st Rhode Island Light, Battery B, Capt. T. Frederick Brown.
4th United States, Battery K, Lieut. John W. Roder.
5th United States, Battery C and I, Lieut. James Gilliss.

FIFTH ARMY CORPS.

Maj. Gen. GOUVERNEUR K. WARREN.

PROVOST GUARD.

12th New York Battalion, Maj. Henry W. Rider.

FIRST DIVISION.

Brig. Gen. CHARLES GRIFFIN.

First Brigade.

Brig. Gen. ROMEYN B. AYERS.

140th New York Col. George Ryan.
146th New York Col. David T. Jenkins.
91st Pennsylvania Lieut. Col. Joseph H. Sinex.
155th Pennsylvania Lieut. Col. Alfred L. Pearson.
2d United States, Companies B, C, F, H, I, and K; Capt. James W. Long.
11th United States, Companies B, C, D, E, F, and G, 1st Battalion; Capt. Francis M. Cooley.
12th United States, Companies A, C, D, and G, 1st Battalion;
12th United States, Companies A, C, D, F, and H, 2d Battalion; } Maj. Luther B. Bruen.
14th United States, 1st Battalion, Capt. Edward Mck. Hudson.
17th United States, Companies A, C, D, G, and H, 1st Battalion;
17th United States, Companies A, B, and C, 2d Battalion; } Capt. James F. Grimes.

Second Brigade.

Col. JACOB B. SWEITZER.

9th Massachusetts; Col. Patrick R. Guiney.
22d Massachusetts*; Col. William S. Tilton.
32d Massachusetts; Col. George L. Prescott.
4th Michigan; Lieut. Col. George W. Lumbard.
62d Pennsylvania; Lieut. Col. James Hull.

Official Records of the War of the Rebellion, Series I, Vol. 36, Part I, p. 109. This page from the *Official Records* lists the command structure for the Fifth Army Corp in May 1884, at the time of the Battle of the Wilderness. The chart lists the various regiments that comprised each of the brigades and identifies the officer who was leading each regiment.

Chapter 5

Historical and Genealogical Societies, Libraries, and Other Archives

You will be amazed at the amount of primary source materials—letters, journals, diaries, and photographs—available in local libraries, historical and genealogical societies, and other archives in the area where your regiment was formed. Also, every state has a historical society, genealogical society, archive for military records, and possibly other sources of collections and materials. For instance, the State House in Boston has a flag preservation project with the flags issued to the various regiments. By contacting them, we obtained slides of the flags for the 18th Massachusetts and a brief text description of each flag. Pennsylvania has a similar flag preservation project, and a book has been published depicting the flags of its regiments.

Start by listing the town or towns from which the regiment was formed, along with any other towns supplying a significant number of men to the regiment. Make sure to include the town where your ancestor lived.

The next step is to find the name, address, and telephone number of any historical society, genealogical society, or library for each of the towns you listed. Your local library may have directories listing these entities, or you can search the Internet telephone directories, as well as relevant websites. A directory of more than 4,000 historical societies can be found at *www.dad dezio.com/society/*. For a listing of public libraries, the St. Joseph County Public Library has created a database: *www.sjcpl.lib.in.us/homepage/Public Libraries/PubLibSrvsGpherWWW.html*.

Perhaps the best source for locating collections in libraries and museums is the National Union Catalog of Manuscript Collections (NUCMC), discussed in Chapter 8 on Other Major Collections. The NUCMC can be serched over the Internet at *lcweb.loc.gov/coll/nucmc*. Other libraries with

Civil War collections can be found by consulting M. L. Young et al., *Directory of Special Libraries* (Detroit: Gale Research Company, 1986).

Draft a form letter similar to the one in Appendix C, mentioning your interest in the specific regiment and asking if the place has any materials pertaining to either your ancestor or the regiment. Then prepare individual letters addressed to each potential source. This is most easily done using a computer. As shown in the sample letter, it also can be helpful to ask whether they can recommend any other places or sources for potential materials relating to the regiment. You will be surprised at how helpful most people will be, especially if their collection includes any such materials.

At these local places, also ask whether there is a town history that discusses the town's role in the Civil War. Most towns have such a history, with at least some discussion of the regiments it helped raise. Some of these histories are very detailed and discuss such things as sending the men off

> It is highly recommended that you send a self-addressed, stamped envelope along with your request. Many local historical societies, libraries, and museums operate on very tight budgets. By sending a stamped return envelope, you almost always will receive a quick response to your inquiry.

to war; ceremonies presenting the regiment with its flag; the effort to send supplies, food, and materiel to the men, and the return of the regiment at the end of its service.

In addition to local sources, there are numerous other sources you should contact. At a minimum, contact your regiment's state's historical society, archive, and genealogical society. Appendix H contains a list of these places, including their addresses, telephone numbers, and, if possible, websites. Send a request letter to each location.

After the Civil War, there was a tremendous movement of people from their hometowns to other locations. Also, from the time of the Civil War to the present, descendants of the soldiers have moved all over the United States and elsewhere. Collections of Civil War letters and documents have passed hands numerous times, some into the collections of far-flung individuals, libraries, universities, and other entities. It is very possible that historical societies and archives of other states have collections pertaining to people from your regiment. Consider sending request letters to many of the state historical societies and archives listed in Appendix H. It is worth the price of the stamps, and you may find a treasure trove of materials in some unlikely place.

Many colleges, universities, and museums also have extensive and excellent collections on the Civil War, including collections pertaining to individuals and specific military units. Appendix L lists some of these sources of materials. We cannot overstate how important these collections are. For the 18th Massachusetts, we have found letters, journals, diaries, and photographs in over a dozen collections. While some of these materials were in collections in the New England area, a few of the best finds were from places as far away as California.

Although numerous historical societies, libraries, and other archives may have relevant materials, to search them all is simply not feasible. Target those that seem the most likely, and follow up on other locations as they become known. Materials at a national park, for example, may lead you to investigate whether some obscure local historical society in another state has materials of interest. Write them a letter, and see where the trail may lead.

It is always a good idea to keep a record of where you found something. Note on your file folders, or somewhere else handy, the sources that provided the materials. If you plan to ever use the information you obtain in a book or other publication, you need to properly cite the source when discussing the material—for example, Letter of Stephen Thomas, dated May 4, 1862, Thomas Collection of the Middleboro Historical Society. Some materials may not be published without the permission of the owner due to copyright law, even though the materials are more than 100 years old. To give credit where credit is due and to follow up on any approvals that may be required, you need to know where you obtained the material. Although you may not presently have any intention of publishing a regimental history, that could change in the future, and making brief notations of sources now may avoid headaches later.

Chapter 6

Historic Sites, Parks, and Battlefields

Many battlefields and national parks have their own archives of manuscripts, letters, photographs, and documents. Many of those operated by the National Park Service have extensive collections. Some may pertain only to the battle fought at that location, but others include entire collections of letters, covering many individuals' entire service throughout the war. Some of the materials may be originals, some may be photocopies, and some may be transcriptions made by park volunteers. In any event, these battlefield parks are excellent sources.

There are many instances where there is no rhyme or reason as to what a specific park will have in its collection, other than that they are trying to preserve anything and everything they can. Thus at Gettysburg National Military Park, you may find a huge collection of letters from someone in your regiment, even though most of the letters pertain to other battles and were written well before or after the battle at Gettysburg. Luck definitely has played a big part in where some of these collections are located.

In the collection at the Manassas National Battlefield Park, Steve found a letter dated June 15, 1880, from his great-great-great-grandfather Stephen Thomas. It seems that the Adjutant General's Office could not find the battle report for the 18th Massachusetts for the Second Battle of Bull Run. As the senior officer at the time of the battle, Stephen Thomas, then a captain, had led the regiment during the battle. In 1880, the Adjutant General's Office contacted him, requesting that he redraft the regiment's report. There in the park's records was a copy of the handwritten report—quite an exciting find!

Appendix I contains a list of the locations, addresses, telephone numbers, and websites of the battlefield parks operated by the National Park

Name: PATRICK GALLIGAN   Rank: PRIVATE

Military Unit: B 18   MA INFANTRY   Grave: 9227

Date of Death: SEP. 19, 1864   Cause: DIARRHEA

Alternate Names: GALLIGHER

Taken Prisoner: 05/05/1864   WILDERNESS, VA

Park Files have Additional Information: NO

Remarks: 09/18/1864 [1]; F. GALLIGHER, GRAVE 8927 [3]

References: p 20 [3]; p 360 [33]

Code Number: 19227

Code Number of 10000 – 29999 = the prisoner was buried at Andersonville.

Code Number of 30000 – 39999 = the prisoner was reported to have died at Andersonville but no burial is recorded.

Code Number of 40000 – 49999 = the prisoner left Andersonville alive.

This document was printed from the database maintained by the Andersonville National Historical Site, which is part of the National Park Service. The database entry identifies the name of the soldier, his regiment, when and where he was taken prisoner, whether he was transferred, and other information. As you would expect, some of the entries are missing quite a bit of information, but many of them, such as this one for Patrick Galligan, are very complete.

Service. This is not an exhaustive list, but it is a good start. There also are many battlefields owned and operated by states, private groups, and even individuals. Unfortunately, some battlefields no longer exist, having fallen victim to development, flooding, or lack of interest. Do some research. You should have little trouble finding the name and address of the organization controlling a specific battlefield. Send a request letter to each place where your regiment may have fought. (For a sample request letter, see Appendix C.)

Visiting the battlefield where your ancestor fought is an awesome experience, especially after you have conducted some research, during which you will have found maps and descriptions that pinpoint the location of your ancestor's regiment. Take along copies of some letters and battle descriptions. Ask the park rangers how to get to the regiment's location and if any markers are present. When you explain what you are doing, they will be almost as excited as you are and will provide whatever assistance they can. When you get to the spot, pull out the letters and read the words of the men who were there, describing their actions and what went on around them. The experience of reading their words while standing where they stood and looking over the ground on which they fought is nothing short of incredible.

Chapter 7

National Archives

The National Archives and Records Administration (NARA) contains what may be the mother lode of documents pertaining to the Civil War. We will be focusing on the portions of the National Archives pertaining to individual men (and women) and their military units.

There are three major collections of records of use in your research: the Compiled Military Service Records (CMSR); the pension records; and the Records of Events documenting the activities of your regiment and each separate company therein. You also may be able to find relevant photographs and maps.

COMPILED MILITARY SERVICE RECORDS

The Compiled Military Service Records (CMSR) were created after the war by the War Department, based upon muster rolls, regimental returns and descriptive books, hospital rolls, and other records turned in to the War Department during and after the war, including records captured from the Confederacy. The CMSR includes military records for both Union and Confederate soldiers, but many of the Confederate records were destroyed during the war or shortly thereafter. Even the Union records have holes in them, as some were lost or destroyed during or after the war. Further, many records that should have been turned in to the government became mementos for private collections.

In general, the military records contain little useful information, although there can be surprises, and you certainly should request the records pertaining to your ancestor. Typically, these records provide very basic information about the soldier's military life, such as whether he was present or absent when roll was taken; date of enlistment; dates of any promotions; whether wounded in battle; hospitalizations; date of discharge; reason for discharge; place of birth; and possibly personal information, such as height, weight, hair and eye color, and occupation. The military records may also contain other miscellaneous documents and information.

PENSION RECORDS

The pension records are much more likely than the military records to contain interesting information regarding your ancestor and the other men in his regiment. On occasion, the material contained in the pension files is nothing short of amazing.

The National Archives do not contain pension records for Confederate forces. This certainly is not surprising, as the U.S. government did not give pensions to Confederate soldiers, sailors, or their families. However, many of the individual states composing the Confederacy did grant pensions to veterans and their families: Alabama, Arkansas, Florida, Georgia, Kentucky, Louisiana, Mississippi, Missouri, North Carolina, Oklahoma, South Carolina, Tennessee, Texas, and Virginia. Pension records can be found in the archives of those states, most of which are listed in Appendix J. Most of this information is also available on the internet.

Pensions were granted to U.S. veterans, their widowed spouses, minor children, and dependent parents. As part of the application process, the applicant had to supply proof of having been in the military during the war; being married to the soldier in question;

Although not necessary for the research being covered by this guide, there are several publications you may find interesting and useful in conducting research into materials held by the National Archives:

Kenneth W. Munden, et al., *The Union: A Guide to Federal Archives Relating to the Civil War* (Washington, DC: National Archives and Records Administration, 1962. Reprint. 1986).

Henry Putney Beers, *The Confederacy: A Guide to Federal Archives Relating to the Civil War* (Washington, DC: National Archives and Records Administration, 1962. Reprint. 1986).

A Guide to Civil War Maps in the National Archives (Washington, DC: National Archives and Records Administration, 1964. Reprint. 1986).

Guide to Genealogical Research in the National Archives (Washington, DC: National Archives and Records Administration, revised 1985).

Guide to Federal Records in the National Archives of the United States, 3 vols. (Washington, DC: National Archives and Records Administration, 1995).

These guides may be purchased by writing to Civil War Guides, National Archives Trust Board, Department 716, P.O. Box 100793, Atlanta, GA 30384, or visiting NARA's website, *www.archives.gov/publications/ nhprc_historical.html.* They likely also could be ordered through one of the large book dealers, such as *www.amazon.com.*

being a minor child of the soldier in question; or being the soldier's parent and being dependent upon that person for support. Generally, the application also had to be notarized or supported by a prominent citizen from the town where the veteran lived, who had personal knowledge of the veteran and/or the applicant.

The pension records are often a gold mine for original records. In researching the pension records for various members of the 18th Massachusetts, we have found that roughly a quarter of the pension files contain such finds as original letters from the soldiers; photographs; details of diseases; medical descriptions of wounds; information on the nature of disabilities; details of a soldier's medical history and death; discussions of a soldier's family and his occupation; what he did after the war; and postwar medical problems. A wealth of information and material generally not available anywhere else!

The pension records also provide a source for locating an ancestor if little is known other than the person's name. All of the Federal pensions are indexed in a series of microfilm materials published by the National Archives and called Publication T288, *General Index to Pension Files, 1861–1934*. This consists of 544 rolls of microfilm, labeled alphabetically by surname. On the microfilm are index cards with each person's name; his unit, including the state it was from; the pension application number; the assigned pension number; and possibly the name of the spouse or other person applying for the pension.

This index is available at the various regional branches maintained by the National Archives (see Appendix K). A list of the microfilm roll numbers also is available on-line at *www.archives.gov/research_room/genealogy/military/pension_index_1861_to_1934.html/#rolllist*. Locate the roll of microfilm on which your ancestor's last name would appear alphabetically.

Copies of the microfilm roll can be rented through the NARA Microfilm Rental Program, with a typical charge of $3.50 per roll, which allows you to rent it for a period of thirty days. For details on this program, see

> There is something eerie about reading the contents of the pension records. First, no one has seen or read those documents in probably a 100 years or longer. In addition, the records often contain a wealth of very personal information regarding health problems, marriages, children, financial difficulties, and other details about the life of the soldier and his family, both during and after the war. Sometimes the descriptions of disabilities, handicaps, and dire financial conditions will make you shake your head in wonder as to how the people survived such ordeals.

www.archives.gov/research_room/obtain_copies/microfilm.html#rent. For additional information on this program, contact National Archives, Census Microfilm Rental Program, P.O. Box 30, 9050 Junction Drive, Annapolis Junction, MD 20701-0030, or call (301) 604-3699.

Alternatively, you can borrow rolls of microfilm through an interlibrary loan program. According to the National Archives, more than 6,000 libraries nationwide participate in this program. To find a participating library near you, call the National Archives at (301) 604-3699. You might want to check first with your local library.

If your ancestor had a common name, you may need to narrow down the list through the process of elimination. The identification of the person's state may be of assistance. You may need to follow up on several possible individuals to determine what part of the state they were from, obtain their pension records, and compare the information gathered to what you already know about your ancestor to determine which is the right person.

If your ancestor served in the Confederate forces, you should be able to conduct a similar search directed to the archives of the state that may have issued a pension to your ancestor or his family members.

RECORDS OF EVENTS

These records are compilations of the activities of the regiments and for each company therein. While some of the records may contain a virtual day-to-day listing of activities, most are more general and merely list such things as where a regiment was stationed and when it moved. Overall, these records lack any real detail or description. For instance, for the 18th Massachusetts, the record of events for August 30, 1862, merely states that it marched to Bull Run and took part in the engagement. Quite a brief summary, to say the least, and it provides the reader with no idea that the regiment was heavily engaged in the battle, losing approximately 60 percent of its men, along with its state flag!

The Records of Events are contained on microfilm, one set for the Union and another set for the Confederate forces: M594, *Compiled Records Showing Service of Military Units in Volunteer Union Organizations* (225 rolls); and M861, *Compiled Records Showing Service of Military Units in Confederate Organizations* (74 rolls).

These records have been published in a ninety-five-volume series: Janet B. Hewett, et al., *Supplement to the Official Records of the Union and Confederate Armies* (Wilmington, NC: Broadfoot Publishing Co., 1994–99). The series can be found in many libraries specializing in Civil War collections, as well as some of the larger university and public libraries.

OBTAINING COPIES OF PENSION AND MILITARY RECORDS

To order copies of pension or military records, you first will need to obtain forms called NATF Form 80. These can be obtained from the regional branches of the National Archives, or from the main facility by writing to National Archives and Records Administration, Attn: NWDT1, 700 Pennsylvania Avenue, NW, Washington, DC 20408-0001. They also can be requested over the Internet at *www.archives.gov/global_pages/contact_us.html*. Provide your name and mailing address, specify that you are requesting Form 80, and state the number of forms you would like.

One form needs to be submitted to request pension records, and another form to request military records, even if they are for the same person. Separate forms need to be submitted for each individual whose records you are requesting.

On the forms, specify that you want "the complete" record. Otherwise, the researchers will send only what they feel to be the most important portion of the file, and this will be limited to twenty to thirty pages. If there are more pages than this, you will be charged extra, but it is worth it. Presently, the standard charge per request is $10.00.

When you complete the forms, keep the pink copies for your file and mail the remainder to National Archives and Records Administration, General Reference Branch (NNRPG-P), 700 Pennsylvania Avenue, NW, Washington, DC 20408-0001. You should receive the records in eight to ten weeks.

PHOTOGRAPHS AND MAPS

An extensive collection of Civil War photographs, maps, drawings, plans, and other pictorial materials is also part of the National Archives. A microfilm catalog is available for the Matthew Brady photographs. To inquire about possible photographs and graphic materials relevant to your regiment, write to Still Picture Reference, Special Media Archives Services Division, National Archives at College Park, 8601 Adelphi Road, College Park, MD 20740-6001, or telephone (301) 713-6625, ext. 234. Copies of the photographs or other materials can then be ordered by using the forms and following the procedures required by the Special Media Archives Services Division.

These materials supposedly can be searched on-line, although we have not had great results with our brief efforts. To search for photographs and maps in the NARA's collection, start with the general site *www.archives.gov* and use its search feature. Although there is a wealth of information available from this site, whether or not you will be able to find what you are looking for is difficult to predict.

ORDER FOR COPIES OF VETERANS RECORDS
(See Instructions page before completing this form)

DATE RECEIVED IN NNRG

INDICATE BELOW THE TYPE OF FILE DESIRED AND THE METHOD OF PAYMENT PREFERRED

1. FILE TO BE SEARCHED (Check one box only)
- ☐ PENSION
- ☐ BOUNTY-LAND WARRANT APPLICATION (Service before 1856 only)
- ☐ MILITARY

2. PAYMENT METHOD (Check one box only)

☐ CREDIT CARD (VISA or MasterCard) for IMMEDIATE SHIPMENT of copies
Account Number:

Exp. Date:

Signature:

Daytime Phone:

☐ BILL ME (No Credit Card)

REQUIRED MINIMUM IDENTIFICATION OF VETERAN - MUST BE COMPLETED OR YOUR ORDER CANNOT BE SERVICED

3. VETERAN (Give last, first, and middle names)

4. BRANCH OF SERVICE IN WHICH HE SERVED
☐ ARMY   ☐ NAVY   ☐ MARINE CORPS

5. STATE FROM WHICH HE SERVED

6. WAR IN WHICH, OR DATES BETWEEN WHICH, HE SERVED

7. IF SERVICE WAS CIVIL WAR,
☐ UNION   ☐ CONFEDERATE

PLEASE PROVIDE THE FOLLOWING ADDITIONAL INFORMATION, IF KNOWN

8. UNIT IN WHICH HE SERVED (Name of regiment or number, company, etc, name of ship)

9. IF SERVICE WAS ARMY, ARM IN WHICH HE SERVED
☐ INFANTRY   ☐ CAVALRY   ☐ ARTILLERY

If other, specify:

Rank
☐ OFFICER   ☐ ENLISTED

10. KIND OF SERVICE
☐ VOLUNTEERS   ☐ REGULARS

11. PENSION/BOUNTY-LAND FILE NO.

12. IF VETERAN LIVED IN A HOME FOR SOLDIERS, GIVE LOCATION (City and State)

13. PLACE(S) VETERAN LIVED AFTER SERVICE

14. DATE OF BIRTH

15. PLACE OF BIRTH (City, County, State, etc.)

18. NAME OF WIDOW OR OTHER CLAIMANT

16. DATE OF DEATH

17. PLACE OF DEATH (City, County, State, etc.)

NATIONAL ARCHIVES TRUST FUND BOARD   NATF Form 80 (rev. 4-92)

DO NOT WRITE BELOW SPACE IS FOR OUR REPLY TO YOU

☐ **NO--We were unable to locate the file you requested above. No payment is required.**

DATE SEARCHED	SEARCHER

☐ **REQUIRED MINIMUM IDENTIFICATION OF VETERAN WAS NOT PROVIDED.** Please complete blocks 3 (give full name), 4, 5, 6, and 7 and resubmit your order.

☐ **A SEARCH WAS MADE BUT THE FILE YOU REQUESTED ABOVE WAS NOT FOUND.** When we do not find a record for a veteran, this does not mean that he did not serve. You may be able to obtain information about him from the archives of the State from which he served.

☐ See attached forms, leaflets, or information sheets.

☐ **YES--We located the file you requested above. We have made copies from the file for you. The cost for these copies is $10.**

DATE SEARCHED	SEARCHER
FILE DESIGNATION	

Make your check or money order payable to NATIONAL ARCHIVES TRUST FUND. Do not send cash. Return this form and your payment in the enclosed envelope to:

NATIONAL ARCHIVES TRUST FUND
P.O. BOX 100221
ATLANTA, GA 30384-0221

PLEASE NOTE: We will hold these copies awaiting receipt of payment for only 45 days from the date completed, which is stamped below. After that time, you must submit another form to obtain photocopies of the file.

THIS IS YOUR MAILING LABEL.

PRESS FIRMLY.

NAME (Last, First, MI)

A547589

STREET

CITY, STATE   ZIP CODE

This is a sample of the NATF Form 80. Filling it out is very easy. Just make sure that you include as much information as possible to identify the person whose records you are requesting.

CONDUCTING RESEARCH AT THE NATIONAL ARCHIVES

Pension and military records can be researched at the National Archives Building, 700 Pennsylvania Avenue, NW, in Washington, DC. Start in Room 400, which is the microfilm reading room. The staff there will be able to answer your questions and get you started.

Pension records and most military records are not available on microfilm. To obtain these files, you fill out request forms identifying the individual and his unit. Three original files may be requested at a time, with a limit of twenty-four in a day.

If you are planning on conducting research at the National Archives, call ahead to confirm the research room hours and have any questions answered. This will avoid wasting valuable research time because you are not familiar with their location or procedures, or have questions that need to be answered. The telephone number for the Consultant's Office is (202) 501-5400. Overall, the staff members at the National Archives are excellent and will go out of their way to be helpful.

As an alternative to conducting this research yourself, you can hire someone to do it for you (see Chapter 2 on Obtaining the Materials). Particularly if you already have identified a list of specific individuals whose files you would like to have researched, this can be a very effective option.

If you have any additional questions about researching at the National Archives, feel free to contact the member of our team who has been involved with the lion's share of our effort, Donald Thompson. He can be contacted through our website, at *www.18thmass.com.*

Chapter 8

Other Major Collections

LIBRARY OF CONGRESS

The Library of Congress has an extensive collection of Civil War materials, including manuscripts and photographs. The catalog can be searched on-line at *www.loc.gov/library*, or you can review materials contained in the Library of Congress by consulting John R. Seller, *Civil War Manuscripts: A Guide to Collections in the Manuscript Division of the Library of Congress* (Washington, DC: Library of Congress, 1986).

The Library of Congress also maintains and operates the National Union Catalog of Manuscript Collections (NUCMC). Using this source, you can find manuscripts in thousands of locations nationwide, including collections held by libraries, historical societies, universities, and other archives. The NUCMC can be searched on-line at *lcweb.loc.gov/coll/nucmc/*. You also can contact the department that operates the NUCMC directly, by writing to Library of Congress, NUCMC Team, 101 Independence Avenue, SE, Washington, DC 20540-4375, or telephoning (202) 707-8419.

In addition to manuscripts, the Library of Congress has a collection of well over 1,000 Civil War photographs of both Union and Confederate officers and enlisted men. Most of these photographs were made by, or under the supervision of, Matthew Brady. In the collection of the James Wadsworth Family Papers, there are an additional 200 photographs. All of these can be searched through the Library of Congress website, *memory.loc.gov/ammem/cwphtml/cwphome.html*, which also provides instructions on how to obtain copies.

U.S. ARMY MILITARY HISTORY INSTITUTE

An extremely important resource is the U.S. Army Military History Institute (MHI), which possesses a tremendous collection of written and photographic materials. Send two letters, one addressed to the Reference

| G | G | G | G | G | P&P Form #67 |

Job Number

Library of Congress
PHOTODUPLICATION SERVICE

ORDER FORM FOR REGULAR PRINTS MADE FROM GLASS NEGATIVE

Instructions: Read "Conditions of Order and Use" on reverse of this form, and sign acknowledgement statement below. Please print or type information. Make check or money order payable to Library of Congress, Photoduplication Service. Credit card payment by Master Card or Visa is accepted. Return white and yellow copies of this form to Library of Congress, Photoduplication Service, Washington, DC 20540-5234. Retain pink copy. For more information call the Photoduplication Service, Public Service Section on (202) 707-5640 or Fax (202) 707-1771.

Date of Request	Customer's Order No.	Deposit Account No. PS-	Customer's Phone No. ( )		
Customer's Name		Office	Reference	Laboratory	
Address					
City, State, Zip Code		**For Office Use Only**			
Attn:					
Delivery Mode: ☐ Customer Pick Up ☐ Mail ☐ Federal Express ☐ Other:					
Delivery Service Customer Account No.	Delivery Address Phone No. ( )	I hereby note and accept the "Conditions of Order and Use" stated on verso of pink copy. If applicable, credit card information is correct and payment will be made.			
If Credit Card Payment: ☐ Master Card ☐ Visa Expiration Date: Credit Card Acct. No.:		Signature:			

GLASS NEGATIVE No.	DESCRIPTION	8 X 10" Glossy	11 X 14" Matte	11 X 14" Glossy	16 X 20" Matte	16 X 20" Glossy	20 X 24" Matte	TOTAL
LC-		*Circle price for size & type of finish desired.*						
		$25	$30	$30	$35	$35	$45	
LC-		$25	$30	$30	$35	$35	$45	
LC-		$25	$30	$30	$35	$35	$45	
LC-		$25	$30	$30	$35	$35	$45	
LC-		$25	$30	$30	$35	$35	$45	
LC-		$25	$30	$30	$35	$35	$45	

SPECIAL INSTRUCTIONS:

PACKAGING AND MAILING FEES

	$20.00 or less	20.01 - 50.00	50.01 - 150.00	over 150.00
US, Canada & Mexico	$8.50	10.50	13.50	10% of Subtotal

For other countries contact the Photoduplication Service for mailing fees.

NOTE: Other delivery options available upon request.

SUBTOTAL	
SURCHARGE	
SUBTOTAL	
PACKAGING & MAILING	
TOTAL	

Delivered To:	Date:

25-70b (12/94)   For prompt, accurate shipment fill in the following mailing label . Please print or type.

The Library of Congress
Photoduplication Service
Washington, DC 20540-5234

Name _____

OFFICIAL BUSINESS
PENALTY FOR PRIVATE USE $300

Order No./Attn. _____

This is the form that you use for ordering prints from the photograph collection of the Library of Congress. As you will see, the costs can add up quickly.

Department, and the other to the Photographic Collection Department, both at U.S. Army Military History Institute, 22 Ashburn Drive, Carlisle Barracks, Carlisle, PA 17013-5008. In both letters, request information regarding the institute's holdings relating to your regiment, and ask about the procedure to use to obtain copies of the materials. The telephone number is (717) 245-3611.

From the MHI's website, *carlisle-www.army.mil/usamhi/*, you can submit requests for information directly. In addition, its document repository is on-line and can be accessed at *carlisle-www.army.mil/usamhi/DL/*. We have used this on-line resource only briefly and did not have a lot of success in finding materials that we already had gotten from the MHI. Our suggestion is that you write or send an e-mail to request a listing of the documentary and photographic materials in their collection that pertain to your regiment.

Chapter 9

Internet Websites

There are tens of thousands of websites dealing with various aspects of the Civil War. Many of these sites are excellent in their scope, thoroughness, and detail. To find websites of interest, we recommend you use *www.google.com*. This site searches over a billion websites to find matches for the terms you enter. It is easy to use and a fantastic way for finding sites of interest.

Another useful search site is AskSam, *www.ask.com*. You enter a question, and it searches for websites fitting your query by using several different search engines. Other useful sites are *www.northernlights.com* and *www.dogpile.com*.

There are thousands of websites pertaining to various aspects of the Civil War. The following are a few sites that deserve special mention and should be given special attention. Many of these websites have links to other sites and categorize the links according to their subject matter.

Another way to find websites is through the use of web rings. These are composed of a series of linked websites, usually all having the same theme. There are hundreds, if not thousands, of web rings pertaining to the Civil War, many of which contain links to numerous websites on regimental histories and information.

CIVIL WAR SOLDIERS AND SAILORS DATABASE

The goal of the Civil War Soldiers and Sailors Database, created by the National Park Service and found at *www.civilwar.nps.gov/cwss/*, is to list every man and woman who served during the Civil War. This will take a while to accomplish, but when completed, it will make finding an ancestor as simple as "query and click."

CIVIL WAR NAVIES

It can be difficult to find information pertaining to the Civil War navies, as most materials focus on the armies. A website that you should find helpful is *www.tarleton.edu/~kjones/navy.html.*

[handwritten: didn't find 8-29-2019]

CIVIL WAR CENTER

The Civil War Center (CWC) at Louisiana State University has created a webpage, *www.cwc.lsu.edu*, with links to thousands of Internet sources. One goal of the CWC is to identify the locations of materials pertaining to regiments. They also are trying to compile all Civil War–related links that can be found on the Internet. The amount of information that is available is staggering in both size and scope. Spending a little time searching through the CWC's site will be well worth it. You may end up finding everything you care to know merely from the links on this site. Have fun!

CYNDI'S LIST

We do not know who Cyndi is, but she has been collecting and grouping website links for as long as anyone. More importantly, she has done a fantastic job of grouping and cataloging these links. At her website, *www.cyndislist.com/cw.htm*, you can spend hours going from link to link and finding a wealth of information. Between this site and the CWC site, you should find a substantial amount of information dealing with your regiment.

OTHER SITES

The following are a few other excellent websites focused on the Civil War:

www.homepages.dsu.edu/jankej/civilwar/civalwar.html is a website run by James Janke, an Assistant Professor at Dakota State University. Among other things, it has dozens of links to other websites, including many libraries and archives.

www.researchonline.net is an excellent source for links to other sites dedicated to various categories of research and materials pertaining to the Civil War, much of it related to the Confederates.

www.ugrr.org/civil/cw-web.htm is a site with several links to other websites related to the Civil War.

www.civilwararchive.com/files.htm is a great website with listings for regimental histories, diaries, and research sources, as well as links to other sites of potential interest.

Chapter 10

Grand Army of the Republic

The GAR was founded in 1866 by veterans who had served in the Union Army. In its day, the GAR was a very powerful political entity, as well as a gathering place for veterans. A private organization, it dissolved in 1956. There were many local chapters of the GAR, and many of their records still survive. When a local chapter closed, and when the GAR dissolved, many of the books and materials were given to local libraries or historical societies. One local historical society had several documents on the 18th Massachusetts titled "War Remembrances." These are large forms on which a soldier entered information about himself, his experiences, and his friends during the war.

There is a central library and information center for the GAR, through which you may be able to locate materials pertaining to the local chapters in the region where your regiment was formed. Write to Grand Army of the Republic, Civil War Museum and Library, Frankford Section, 4278 Griscom Street, Philadelphia, PA 19124, or telephone (215) 289-6484.

The following are other locations with an extensive collection of GAR material and information:

Fire Museum of Trenton
244 Perry Street
Trenton, NJ 08618
(609) 989-4038

GAR Memorial Hall
The Chicago Public Library
400 South State Street
Chicago, IL 60605
(312) 747-4022
www.chipublib.org

New England Civil War Museum
Thomas J. O'Connell Library
14 Park Place
Vernon, CT 06066

Soldiers and Sailors Memorial Hall
4141 5th Avenue
Pittsburgh, PA 15213
(412) 621-4253
soldiersandsailorshall.org

Wisconsin Veterans Museum
30 West Mifflin Street, Room 200
Madison, WI 53702
(608) 266-1680

Chapter 11

Books

It seems as though there are a million books dealing with the Civil War, and the list is constantly expanding. Finding what is useful to your research can seem like an overwhelming task. But there is a simple method to zero in on information pertaining to your regiment. The books that will be most useful fall into three categories: the *Official Records;* compendiums and bibliographies that identify books, articles, and other materials on specific regiments; and books on specific battles and campaigns.

THE *OFFICIAL RECORDS*

The *Official Records,* or *O.R.,* as they often are called, refers to a 128-volume series of books by the U.S. War Department, *War of the Rebellion: A Compilation of the Official Records of the Union and Confederate Armies* (Washington, DC: Government Printing Office, 1880–1900), which includes battle reports and correspondence of Union and Confederate regiments. In this guide, although technically incorrect, we are using the term *Official Records* to refer collectively to the following series as well:

U.S. War Department, *Atlas to Accompany the Official Records of the War of Rebellion* (Washington, DC: Government Printing Office, 1891–95).

U.S. Naval War Records Office, *War of the Rebellion: A Compilation of the Official Records of the Union and Confederate Navies,* 30 vols. (Washington, DC: Government Printing Office, 1874–1922).

Janet B. Hewett, et al., *Supplement to the Official Records of the Union and Confederate Armies,* 95 vols. (Wilmington, NC: Broadfoot Publishing Co., 1994–99).

U.S. Adjutant General's Office, *Official Army Register of the Volunteer Force of the United States Army, 1861–1865* (Washington, DC: Adjutant General's Office, 1865).

These books can be found in most major libraries, both public and at colleges and universities. Recently there has been an effort to republish these

books, and they even can be purchased on CD-ROMs. If you do a
little searching on the Internet, you
will find some sites that have summaries, indexes, and sometimes
even full-text sections of the *Official
Records* available on-line. In time,
the entire text of all these series
likely will be available on-line.

The *Official Records* contain a
lot of information and material,
particularly the battle reports filled
out by the regimental, brigade, and
division commanders. If your
ancestor was an officer involved in
battle, it is possible you will find
him referenced somewhere in the
Official Records. These materials
will provide you with a detailed
overview of the organization of the
army and its changes over time,
such as which regiments were in
the same brigade as yours and the
names of the officers in command.
There also are maps detailing the

> When purchasing a CD-ROM, you should shop around. The vari-ous companies selling the CD-ROMs offer different options, volumes, and extras. The ability to search and then copy and paste text from the CD-ROM is an invaluable option that can save you hours of time. The Guild Press of Indiana recently released a series of materials on CD-ROM at prices that are fantastic. For instance, the entire 128 volumes of the *Official Records* are on a single CD-ROM, priced at $69.95. The *Atlas of the Official Records of the Civil War,* with 179 color plates, 800 maps, and hundreds of drawings, costs $59.95. The entire 52-volume set of the *Southern Histori-cal Society Papers* is on a single CD-ROM for $69.95. Other collections are also available on CD-ROM. Contact the Guild Press of Indiana, 10655 Andrade Drive, Zionville, IN 46077, (800) 913-9563, *www.guildpress.com.*

movements of the armies during the various campaigns and battles.

While searching through the *Official Records,* keep in mind that reports
by other regiments in your brigade may contain valuable information and
descriptions relevant to your regiment. For instance, we have found that
some commanders included sketches for the line of battle, with identification
of each regiment in the line. Other reports discuss the regiments that fought
alongside them. For the 18th Massachusetts, there are several instances
where the battle reports are either missing or lacking in detail. But through
the reports of other regiments in the same brigade, we have been able to fill
in many pertinent details of the 18th Massachusetts' actions.

Once you find the *Official Records* at a nearby library, be prepared to
spend several hours locating references to your regiment and then copying
the material on the photocopier. Take along several rolls of quarters!

When you are done, the effort will have been well worth the time. Just
with the materials you find in the *Official Records,* you will be able to trace

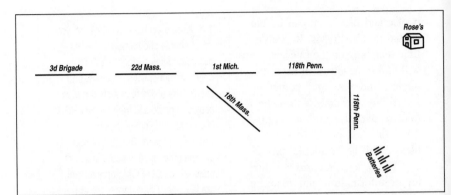

Official Records of the War of the Rebellion. Series I, Vol. 27, Part 1, p. 607. This
report by Colonel Tilton includes a great drawing showing the location and orientation of various regiments, including the 18th Massachusetts at the battle of
Gettysburg. At the Gettysburg National Park, we found a monument dedicated
to the 18th Massachusetts and stone markers that were placed to indicate the
positions for the right and the left of the regiment's line of battle. Using Colonel
Tilton's drawing, it was easy to orient ourselves to where the various regiments
were located and how they were facing during that part of the battle.

your ancestor's regiment through the war and have a good understand-
ing of where it was, what it did, and when.

COMPENDIUMS AND BIBLIOGRAPHIES
Compendiums provide a brief description or set of facts pertaining to each
regiment. All you do is look up your particular regiment. These summaries
typically state such things as when the regiment was formed, when it was
discharged from service, what battles it fought in, maybe some information
on casualties, and other miscellaneous facts. The following are some of the
better known compendiums that should be available through your local
library system:

Frederick H. Dyer, *A Compendium of the War of the Rebellion,* 3 vols.
(New York: Thomas Yoseloff, 1959. Reprint. Dayton: Press of Morningside,
1994). This is perhaps the most famous of the compendiums, and many people will recommend this source during the course of your research.

Stewart Sifakis, *Compendium of the Confederate Armies,* 11 vols. (New
York: Facts on File, 1992–97).

John Wright, *Compendium of the Confederacy,* 2 vols. (Wilmington,
NC: Broadfoot Publishing Company, 1989).

Return of Casualties in the Union forces, &c.–Continued.

BATTLE OF THE WILDERNESS, MAY 5-7, 1864–Continued

Command.	Killed.		Wounded.		Captured or missing.		Aggregate.
	Officers.	Men.	Officers.	Men.	Officers.	Men.	
FIFTH ARMY CORPS.							
MAJ. GEN. GORVERNEUR K. WARREN.							
PROVOST GUARD.							
12th New York Battalion							
FIRST DIVISION.							
BRIG. GEN. CHARLES GRIFFIN.							
First Brigade.							
BRIG. GEN. ROMEVN B. AVRES.							
Staff................					1		1
140th New York	1	22	5	113	5	109	255
146th New York	3	17	5	62	6	219	312
91st Pennsylvania				9		2	11
155th Pennsylvania		7	2	40		6	55
2d United States			1				1
11th United States	2	9	2	23		19	65
12th United States		15	4	47		43	110
14th United States		4	5	74	1	34	118
17th United States		1	1	6			8
Total First Brigade	6	73	25	384	14	432	936
Second Brigade.							
COL. JACOB B. SWEITZER.							
9th Massachusetts	3	23	9	99		3	137
22d Massachusetts		5	1	33		3	42
32d Massachusetts				16		3	19
4th Michigan		5	4	29		4	42
62d Pennsylvania		8		47	1	5	61
Total Second Brigade	3	41	14	221	1	18	301
Third Brigade.							
BRIG. GEN. JOSEPH J. BARLETT.							
26th Maine	1	12	2	80		16	111
18th Massachusetts		8	3	24		29	61
1st Michigan	1	4	3	44		12	64
16th Michigan		3		37			40
44th New York	1	3	1	61		1	67
82d Pennsylvania		13		59		24	100
118th Pennsylvania		2	1	37		25	65
Total Third Brigade	3	47	12	342		107	511
Total First Division	12	163	51	950	15	557	1,748
SECOND DIVISION.							
BRIG. GEN. JOHN C. ROBINSON.							
First Brigade.							
COL. SAMUEL H. LEONARD							
COL. PETER LYLE.							
16th Maine				19	1	20	40
19th Massachusetts			2	8		1	11
24th Massachusetts		5		12			17
104th New York				2			2
Total First Brigade		5	2	41	1	21	70

Official Records of the War of the Rebellion, Series I, Vol. 36, Part 1, p. 123. This chart lists the casualties sustained by each regiment during the Battle of the Wilderness. With information from the rosters, you should be able to identify most, if not all, of the individual soldiers who were listed as killed, wounded, captured, or missing in action. Particularly from the pension records, you are often able to learn additional details, such as precisely where a soldier was wounded. We use our database to track all of this information and to make it available for searching and generating reports.

United Confederate Veterans, *List of Organized Camps of the United Confederate Veterans* (New Orleans: Rogers' Printing Co., 1921).

William F. Fox, *Regimental Losses in the American Civil War 1861–1865,* 18th ed. (Dayton: Morningside House, 1985). Though this source does not provide information as to the battles specific regiments were involved in, it does provide a listing of casualties for each regiment and other details, such as the type of weapon the regiment used.

George Lang, et al., comp., *Medal of Honor Recipients, 1863–1994,* 2 vols. (New York: Facts on File, 1995). This source provides a listing of Medal of Honor recipients. During the Civil War, it was typical for a person who captured a Confederate flag to be awarded the Medal of Honor. It also was awarded for courage during battle.

Bibliographies are collections of references to published (and in some cases, nonpublished) works pertaining to individual units. For instance, Charles Dornbusch's work showed that there were several articles on the 18th Massachusetts written by Amasa Guild and published in the *Dedham Historical Register* in 1902. To use these books, simply look up your regiment. You may need some assistance deciphering the locations of the sources, but the reference librarian should be able to help. All of the following sources are widely available:

Charles E. Dornbusch, *Military Bibliography of the Civil War,* 4 vols. (vol. 1–3, New York: New York Public Library, 1971–87; vol. 4, Dayton: Press of Morningside, 1987) This is a guide to published regimental histories, both Union and Confederate.

Myron J. Smith, Jr., *American Civil War Navies: A Bibliography* (Metuchen, NJ: Scarecrow Press, Inc., 1972). For some reason, Dornbusch's work does not include the U.S. Navy. So if you are researching someone who was in the navy, take a look at Smith's bibliography for possible materials of interest.

Harold L. Cole, *Civil War Eyewitnesses: An Annotated Bibliography of Books and Articles, 1955–1986* (Columbia, SC: University of South Carolina Press, 1988). This bibliography covers firsthand accounts of the war.

Thomas Broadfoot. *Civil War Books: A Priced Checklist with Advice,* 5th ed. (Wilmington, NC: Broadfoot Publishing Co., 2000).

Lee W. Meredith. *Guide to Civil War Periodicals,* 2 vols. (Twentynine Palms, CA: Historical Indexes, 1991 and 1996). This is an index of articles and reviews published from 1983 to 1996.

Eugene C. Murdock. *The Civil War in the North: A Selective Annotated Bibliography* (New York: Garland Publishing, 1987). This book provides summaries and indexes to approximately 5,600 books, essays, and articles.

Allan Nevins, et al., *Civil War Books: A Critical Bibliography,* 2 vols. (Baton Rouge: Louisiana State University Press, 1967).

If possible, search each of these references. You may be surprised at the number of articles and books that include information on your regiment. Once you have gathered a listing of sources, you are ready to find and obtain copies of the materials. Libraries with large Civil War collections may have some or all of the sources you have found. Others may be available for purchase though book dealers, or you may be able to obtain copies by contacting a local historical society or library. Good luck!

BOOKS ON SPECIFIC BATTLES AND CAMPAIGNS

Particularly in recent years, there have been a number of excellent books published dealing with specific campaigns and battles. In addition to telling the story, these books often include a very detailed index and, best of all, copious footnotes identifying and documenting the sources used by the author. These are fantastic sources for locating materials pertaining to your regiment.

Take your list of battles and the charts of the command structure, and head to a large bookstore. Go to the Civil War section and pull up a chair. Starting at the beginning of the section, look for books on the battles in which your regiment fought. Turn to the index of each book and look up your regiment, the name of your regiment's commander, the name of your brigade's commander, and the name of your division's commander. Then look up the pages indicated. At the least, you should get an overview of what your

As your research progresses, you probably will be able to identify some of the specific regiments your ancestor fought against during a battle. It can be very interesting to do a search on any opposing regiments to learn what they had to say about the battle.

At the second battle of Bull Run, the 18th Massachusetts was involved in the charge on the unfinished railroad cut. Decimated during the attack (the regiment sustained 169 casualties out of the 320 men present), the regiment fell back, leaving its state colors behind. When the flag was returned to Massachusetts in 1900, there was a tag attached to it stating that it had been captured by the 27th Virginia, one of the regiments opposing the 18th Massachusetts at the railroad cut. The capture of the flag is not mentioned in the recently published history for this regiment, however. This omission may be due to the fact that few men of the 27th Virginia survived the war, and there are only a few incomplete collections of letters from those who served in the regiment.

regiment likely did during the battle. If you are lucky, you will find specific mentions of your regiment. For any reference to your regiment, see if there are any footnotes identifying the sources used by the author. If so, write them down so that you can follow up and find copies of those materials.

If your regiment fought at Gettysburg, there are several excellent books that have been written:

Edwin B. Coddington, *The Gettysburg Campaign: A Study in Command* (New York: Charles Scribner's Sons, paperback edition, 1984).

Harry W. Pfanz, *Gettysburg: The Second Day* (Chapel Hill: University of North Carolina Press, 1987).

Harry W. Pfanz, *Gettysburg: Culp's Hill and Cemetery Hill* (Chapel Hill: University of North Carolina Press, 1993).

Jeffry D. Wert, *Gettysburg: Day Three* (New York: Simon and Shuster, 2001).

If your regiment was at the second battle of Bull Run (or Manassas, depending on your orientation), you should look at the following:

John J. Hennessey, *Return to Bull Run: The Campaign and Battle of Second Manassas* (New York: Simon & Schuster, 1993).

Some other excellent books with detailed biographical references and citations to specific regiments pertaining to specific battles are as follows:

William C. Davis, *Battle of Bull Run,* 2nd ed. (Mechanicsburg, PA: Stackpole Books, 1995).

Ernest B. Furgurson, *Chancellorsville 1863* (New York: Vintage Books, 1992).

Gary W. Gallagher, *The Spotsylvania Campaign* (Chapel Hill: University of North Carolina Press, 1998).

James Lee McDonough, *Shiloh: In Hell before Night* (Knoxville: University of Tennessee Press, 1977).

Stephen W. Sears, *Chancellorsville* (New York: Houghton Mifflin Co., 1996).

Stephen W. Sears, *To the Gates of Richmond: The Peninsula Campaign* (New York: Houghton Mifflin Co., 1996).

William L. Shea and Earl J. Hess, *Pea Ridge: Civil War Campaigns in the West* (Chapel Hill: University of North Carolina Press, 1992).

Noah Andre Trudeau, *The Last Citadel: Petersburg, Virginia, June 1864–April 1865* (Baton Rouge: Louisiana State University Press, 1991).

David A. Welker. *Tempest at Ox Hill: The Battle of Chantilly* (Cambridge, MA: Da Capo Press, 2002).

Jeffry D. Wert, *From Winchester to Cedar Creek: The Shenandoah Campaign of 1864* (Mechanicsburg, PA: Stackpole Books, 1997).

In addition to books dealing with specific battles, you may be able to find a history that was written on the corps of which your regiment was a part. If your regiment was part of the Union's V Corps, you should take a look at this book:

William H. Powell, *The Fifth Army Corps* (Reprint. Dayton: Press of Morningside Bookshop, 1984).

Interestingly, Steve went to his local library for a copy of Powell's *The Fifth Army Corps* and, through an interlibrary loan, was furnished an original copy published in 1896. This copy had been owned by a J. L. Smith, who was a soldier in the 118th Pennsylvania, which was in the same brigade as the 18th Massachusetts. Smith had made several notations in the margins of the book with his comments on Powell's descriptions. He even made a correction on page 636, in footnote 1, where Powell incorrectly identified Smith's name as "J. E. Smith."

Chapter 12

Newspapers

Newspapers constantly followed and reported on the progress of the war. Many of the major newspapers and periodicals had correspondents assigned to specific military units. While most of this reporting covered the "big picture," such as battles and troop movements, there are many mentions of specific regiments and individuals.

In addition to the major news publications, the local newspapers published a tremendous amount of information pertaining to the men and regiments from their town or local area. Some soldiers wrote to the editors of their local papers and provided ongoing updates on what they and their regiments were doing. Some papers even had regular columns written by soldiers local to the area. In addition, local papers often reprinted letters written by soldiers to their family and friends.

Researching newspapers for articles written by or about the men of your regiment is still fairly difficult, although there are projects under way to collect this material and place it on the Internet. At the moment, however, about the best you can do is to identify what local newspapers existed for the towns where your regiment was formed, and then contact them to find out if their papers from 1861 to 1865 still exist and, if so, how you can access them. Many are on microfilm, and almost all of the newspapers require that you view the microfilm or papers yourself to find the information you want. Usually the microfilm is not available through interlibrary loan, so you will need to view it at the newspaper's office or at a local library or historical society.

During our research on the 18th Massachusetts, we were very fortunate to find a large number of newspaper articles written by a sergeant for a local paper in the collections of the Fredericksburg and Spotsylvania National Military Park. We also have found smaller groupings of articles, written by other men in the regiment, in other collections at local historical societies. In general, these articles have been fantastic finds, full of detail and covering a wide range of subjects, from a court-martial to the regiment's glee club.

So far, we have been able to find only a few newspapers that can be searched over the Internet: the *Charleston Mercury,* the *New York Herald,* and the *Richmond Enquirer.* Full-text searches of these papers are available through at least two separate websites: *etext.lib.virginia.edu/helpsheets/ civilwar.html* and *lib.harvard.edu/e-resources/details/c/civilwar.html.*

To find out about additional work being done to place newspapers and periodicals from the Civil War on the Internet, you may want to check with the local newspapers. For more general information, write to the Electronic Text Center, Alderman Library, University of Virginia, Charlottesville, VA 22903, or telephone (804) 924-3230.

Large public libraries tend to have collections of local newspapers, as well as many major newspapers. These usually are on microfilm, but often are not indexed in any meaningful way. Reviewing these materials on microfilm can be tedious. Be prepared for this to take some time, and don't give up. Tom recently pored over four years of papers from a small newspaper, finding almost nothing of relevance. Just when he was about to give up, he ran into an extensive collection of letters from one of the men in the 18th Massachusetts. These were letters the soldier had written to his parents and were full of details on the soldier, his friends, and the regiment.

By searching on the Internet, you may stumble upon a website that contains a wealth of letters pertaining to your regiment. For instance, we found a site created by Tom Hayes, *www.letterscivilwar.com*, where hundreds, if not thousands, of newspaper articles pertaining to the various regiments and military units raised by the commonwealth of Massachusetts have been transcribed and published. If you are researching a Massachusetts regiment, you must check out this site. Other individuals likely are making similar efforts to publish articles from newspapers of other states; such websites provide access to a fantastic amount of material that is very difficult to obtain.

As with all materials, when you find an article of interest, keep track of where you found it. List the name of the publication, the date, and the page. This will make it easy to find for possible future reference and will allow you to properly cite the source of the material.

Chapter 13

Dealers, Retailers, and Auctions

Over the course of several years, we have been able to obtain original photographs, letters, military documents, and other items through auctions and dealers. Some of the items available were too expensive, but many others have been well within our price range. These include an identified frock coat, an identification badge, and a straight razor inscribed as belonging to Col. James Barnes. The three of us met through bidding on a CDV of a sergeant in the 18th Massachusetts. After the auction, we sent e-mails back and forth inquiring as to the others' interest in the photo and the regiment.

Even if you lose the bidding war in an auction, try sending an e-mail to the successful bidder, asking about his or her interest in the item. We have met a number of people interested in the 18th Massachusetts, some of whom were descendants of men in the regiment. A few had collections of materials they were willing to share. Most people will be willing to send you a copy of a photograph or document.

There are several publications that are excellent sources for locating dealers and placing want ads. The subscription rates generally are very reasonable, and these publications attract a wide range of readers.

The Civil War News
Route 1, Box 36
Tunbridge, VT 05077
(800) 222-1861
civilwarnews.com

Civil War Courier
2507 Delaware Avenue
Buffalo, NY 14216

(800) 418-1861
www.civilwarcourier.com

Blue & Gray Magazine
522 Norton Road
Columbus, OH 43228
(614) 870-1861
www.bluegraymagazine.com/2.html

Civil War Times Illustrated
6405 Flank Drive
Harrisburg, PA 17112
www.civilwartimes.com

We have written to many Civil War dealers over the years, telling them that we are interested in the 18th Massachusetts and asking them to contact us if they run across anything from the regiment. This is a long-shot approach, but things come up every now and then, so you should not rule it out. Many dealers keep lists of people interested in specific regiments, and then check the lists when they pick up something of interest (after all, it's always nice to have a buyer virtually lined up before they make an acquisition).

There are several book dealers who publish and specialize in the Civil War. The following two have extensive collections of books pertaining to the Civil War, and both have devoted significant efforts to reprinting books of interest, as well as publishing newly written books.

Broadfoot Publishing Company
1907 Buena Vista Circle
Wilmington, NC 28411
(910) 686-4816
www.broadfootpublishing.com/index.html

Morningside Bookshop
260 Oak Street
Dayton, OH 45410
(937) 461-6736
www.morningsidebooks.com

CERTIFICATE

To be given to Enlisted Men at the time of their Discharge, to enable them to receive part of their pay, &c.

I Certify, on honor, that *James H. Brown* a *Private* of Captain *Thos. Weston* Company (*E*) of the *18th* Regiment of *Mass* Volunteers, of the State of *Massachusetts*, born in *East Bridgewater* State of *Massachusetts*, aged *30* years, *5* feet *10½* inches high, *dark* complexion, *grey* eyes, *brown* hair, and by occupation *shoemaker*, having joined the Company on its original organization at *Duxbury Mass*, and enrolled in it at the muster into the service of the United States at *Duxbury Mass* on the *twenty third* day of *May*, 186*1*, (or was mustered in service as a recruit by _____ at _____, on the _____ day of _____, 186___, to serve in the Regiment,) for the term of *three years unless sooner discharged* and having served honestly and faithfully with his Company in *Virginia* to the present date, is now entitled to a Discharge, by reason of Surgeon's Certificate of Disability.

The said *James H. Brown* has only a partial descriptive roll, and the amount of pay and allowances due him cannot be correctly ascertained. He has pay due him from the *31st* day of *October*, 186*2* the date of the muster last preceding his entry into hospital, to the present date; and he is entitled to pay and subsistence for travelling to place of enrollment, and whatever other allowances are authorized to enlisted men so discharged. Since his entry into hospital, he has received *Four* 0³/100 dollars, advanced by the United States on account of clothing.

This Certificate to be without prejudice to the right of said enlisted man, to whatever additional pay and allowances may hereafter be found due him.

Given in duplicate, at *Genl Hospl Fairfax Seng* this *sixteenth* day of *December*, 186*2* *By order of Brig Genl Wadsworth*

Daniel P. Smith
Surgeon in charge

NOTE.—Two of these certificates (or duplicates) are to be given to each volunteer soldier who may be discharged previously to the discharge of his company, that he may at once receive from the Paymaster the pay, &c., due him; and the captain or other officer commanding the company will certify to the act of the delivery of the duplicate certificates. On these certificates the soldier is " entitled to" his *discharge*, and should also present his discharge to the Paymaster to have the payment endorsed on it. The discharge is to be given back to the soldier by the Paymaster, the latter only retaining as his voucher the duplicate certificates.

PHILP & SOLOMONS, Army Stationers.

This is a typical type of document that you will find through dealers and auctions. This is the Certificate of Discharge for James Brown and provides some interesting information, such as details regarding his physical appearance and occupation.

For original or hard-to-find books, you may need to resort to dealers in antiques and old books. There are many of them, and you can find them with a little searching.

On-line auctions are a great way to find items relating to your regiment. Of the various on-line auctions, *www.ebay.com* is still the best. You even can create a list of search terms for items you are interested in, and eBay will send you an e-mail to let you know when something has been listed that fits your search criteria. We use three different searches: 18 MA, 18 MASS, and 18 MASSA-CHUSETTS. These seem to cover the ground pretty well. Whether you actually get an item or not will depend on your bid. Browse through the Civil War listings on a regular basis: Some amazing things pop up, even though you might not be interested in owning them or able to afford them.

We have obtained some excellent photographs, documents, and personal items identified to various men from our regiment. Any time you are buying or bidding on an item pertaining to your regiment, exercise some caution and common sense. The cost of Civil War items has greatly increased in the past few years, with the price of items identified to a specific soldier increasing even more. Double-check whether the identified person actually was in your regiment. We ran into one photograph being auctioned that was identified as an officer from the 18th Massachusetts. On researching the name, we found that the officer was not part of the 18th Massachusetts, but instead had been with the 15th Massachusetts—an easy mistake for the seller to make. These errors are not limited to dealers selling items. A local historical society has a picture identified as a sergeant with the 18th Massachusetts. While the person named *was* in the regiment, he never, to our knowledge, obtained a rank higher than private.

CDV of 1st Sgt. Thomas Childs, Co. E, 18th Massachusetts. This is the photograph that both Donald and Steve were bidding on over eBay and, after the bidding was over, resulted in Steve joining his research efforts with those of Donald and Tom.

Chapter 14

Reenactments and Shows

If you are lucky, you may be researching a regiment that has an active reenactment group. If this is the case, you may have a wealth of resources available to help with your research. Generally, one or more people in the reenactment group will have conducted research on the regiment, and even if this is not the case, you will find a group of people interested in assisting you (as long as you do not mind sharing your research).

You may find Civil War shows to be another source for materials relating to your regiment. At these shows, you will find dozens and dozens of vendors selling Civil War items, ranging from museum-quality items to decrepit relics. You may possibly find original materials relating to your regiment, but that may be a bit overly optimistic. Nevertheless, ask the dealers to keep an eye out for items pertaining to your regiment; you may get an unexpected phone call telling you of an item that has turned up.

Some planning will help make your trip to a show more successful. Before the show, put together a list of the regiments in your brigade, the names of the reg-

Steve attended a show in the Philadelphia area and gave his card to several dealers who kept lists of people looking for materials on specific regiments. About a year later, he received a call from one of the dealers, who recently had picked up a straight razor that had inscribed on one side of the bone handle, "Col. James Barnes," and on the other side "18th Mass. Inf. 1862."

Whether an item is genuine is always a question you will face. Particularly with the skyrocketing value of identified items, some unscrupulous individuals have been known to inscribe names on items—particularly military items such as guns, swords, uniforms, and cartridge boxes—and try to pass them off as genuine. With the straight razor, Steve had no reason to doubt its genuineness and felt the price was very reasonable, so he purchased it.

imental commanders, and a listing of the battles they were engaged in. Take along some business cards or small papers with your name, address, telephone number, and the identity of your regiment.

Go early in the day, before the crowds arrive. Take a quick tour of the facility, noting which dealers may have items of possible interest. Many of the dealers will be selling guns, swords, and items not identified to either a regiment or an individual. Note on a chart where the dealers of interest are located, so you can find them easily later. After your general tour, now the fun begins. Visit every dealer of interest, and tell him or her that you are looking for items related to your regiment. Even if someone does not have anything, he or she may be able to direct you to another dealer who does. Many dealers know the stock of their fellow dealers as well as they know their own. Dealers in photographs, letters, maps, and books probably present the best chance of finding something relating to your regiment.

Closing Thoughts

Researching an ancestor in the Civil War is a very rewarding experience. You are uncovering and preserving a part of your family history, usually a part that has long been forgotten. What you learn through the research will give you insight into the motivations of the men in your regiment, how they dealt with the tremendous adversity presented by the war, and many other details of their lives.

This type of research also makes the Civil War a much more personal experience. Rather than focusing on the big picture, you are looking at a very small cog in the wheel, generally composed of regular people, with ordinary problems and concerns, who found themselves swept into a turning point in American history.

We truly hope you have found this research guide to be helpful. The methods we have suggested and the sources we have listed are tried and true. Any amateur historian can undertake the same kind of research we did. The materials exist. All it takes is enough interest to invest the necessary effort, and success is virtually guaranteed.

If you have any questions or comments, whether about information in this book or some other avenue for conducting research, we would like to hear from you. Tom has created a website for the 18th Massachusetts, named appropriately enough *www.18thMass.com*. Please feel free to contact us through the website. Let us know if this book has been helpful to you or if you have any suggestions that would make it better.

We wish you the best of luck with your own research.

Stephen McManus
Donald Thompson
Thomas Churchill

Appendix A

Correspondence Tracking

Date	To Whom	Received Response?

Appendix B

Checklist of Places or Organizations Contacted

Name of Organization/Place Contacted	Date Contacted	Rec. Response?

Appendix C

Sample Request Letter

1234 S. Main Street
Media, PA 19063
(610) 555-1212
August 30, 2002

Historian
Dedham Historical Society
South Street
Dedham, MA 02346

Re: 18th Massachusetts Volunteer Infantry

Dear Sir/Madam:

I am writing to inquire as to whether the Dedham Historical Society has any materials in its collection pertaining to a specific Civil War regiment, the 18th Massachusetts.

I have been interested in this regiment for quite some time. My great-great-great-grandfather, Stephen Thomas, was the captain of Company D. Very little has been written about the 18th Massachusetts, and I have been conducting research in an effort to locate copies of letters, diaries, journals, photographs, and other materials pertaining to the regiment.

It would be greatly appreciated if you could let me know whether the Historical Society has any such materials in its collection. If so, please let me know how I can obtain copies or transcriptions of them.

Finally, I welcome any suggestions you can make as to other potential sources I might contact to locate information or materials pertaining to the regiment.

Thank you for your assistance. I look forward to hearing from you.

Sincerely,

Stephen M. McManus

Appendix D

Sources for Rosters

BOOKS
General Sources

Hewett, Janet B. *The Roster of Confederate Soldiers, 1861–1865*. 16 vols. Wilmington, NC: Broadfoot Publishing Company, 1995–96.

The Roster of Union Soldiers, 1861–1865. 33 vols. Wilmington, NC: Broadfoot Publishing Company, 1996–2001.

Alabama

Brewer, Willis. *Alabama, Her History, Resources, War Records, and Public Men (1872)*.

Arkansas

Arkansas Confederate Veterans and Widows Pension Applications.

California

Adjutant General. *Records of California Men in the War of the Rebellion, 1861 to 1867*. Sacramento, CA: J. D. Young, Supt. State Printing, 1890.

Connecticut

General Assembly. *Record of Service of Connecticut Men in the Army and Navy of the United States during the War of the Rebellion*. Hartford, CT: Case, Lockwood & Brainard, 1889.

Adjutant General's Office. *Errata*.

Florida

Board of State Institutions. *Soldiers of Florida in the Seminole Indian, Civil and Spanish American Wars*. Live Oak, FL: Democrat Book and Job Print, 1903.

Hartman, David W. *Biographical Rosters of Florida's Confederate and Union Soldiers, 1861–1865*. 6 vols. Wilmington, NC: Broadfoot Publishing Company, 1995.

Florida CSA Pension Applications.

Georgia

Confederate Pension and Record Department. *Roster of the Confederate Soldiers of Georgia, 1861–1865.* 7 vols. Hapeville, GA: Longino & Porter, 1955–58.

Illinois

Adjutant General. *Roster of Officers and Enlisted Men.* 9 vols. Springfield, IL: Adjutant General's Office, 1900.

Indiana

Adjutant General. *Report of the Adjutant General of the State of Indiana, 1861–1865.* 8 vols. Indianapolis, IN: Holloway, 1865–66.

Iowa

Adjutant General. *Roster and Record of Iowa Soldiers in the War of Rebellion.* 6 vols. Des Moines, IA: English, 1910.

Kansas

Adjutant General. *Report of the Adjutant General of the State of Kansas, 1861–65.* Topeka, KS: Hudson, 1896.

Kentucky

Adjutant General. *Confederate Kentucky Volunteers War, 1861–65.* 2 vols. Frankfort, KY: State Journal, 1915.

Adjutant General. *Report of the Adjutant General of the State of Kentucky, 1861–65.* 2 vols. Frankfort, KY: State Journal, 1866.

Index of Kentucky Confederate Pension Applications.

Louisiana

Booth, Andrew B. *Records of Louisiana Confederate Soldiers and Louisiana Confederate Commands.* 3 vols. New Orleans, 1920. Reprint. Spartanburg, SC: The Reprint Company, 1984.

Maine

Adjutant General. *Annual Report of the Adjutant General of the State of Maine.* 3 vols. Augusta, ME: Stevens & Sayward, 1862, 1863, 1866.

Maryland

The General Assembly. *Maryland Volunteers, War of 1861–65.* 2 vols. Baltimore, MD: Guggenheimer, Weil, 1899.

Maryland in the Civil War: The South.

Massachusetts

Adjutant General. *Massachusetts Soldiers, Sailors, and Marines in the Civil War.* 9 vols. Norwood, MA: Norwood, 1931.

Record of the Massachusetts Volunteers, 1861–1865. 2 vols.

Michigan

Legislature. *Record of Service of Michigan Volunteers in the Civil War, 1861–1865.* 46 vols. Kalamazoo, MI: Everard, 1903.

Minnesota

Board of Commissioners. *Minnesota in the Civil and Indian Wars, 1861–1865.* St. Paul, MN: Pioneer Press, 1890.

Mississippi

1890 Mississippi Index of Civil War Veterans and Their Widows.

New Hampshire

Legislature. *Revised Register of the Soldiers and Sailors of New Hampshire in the War of the Rebellion, 1861–1865.* Concord, NH: Evans, 1895.

New Jersey

Adjutant General. *Record of the Officers and Men of New Jersey in the Civil War, 1861–65.* 2 vols. Trenton, NJ: Murphy, 1876.

New York

Legislature. *Report of the Adjutant General.* 43 vols. Albany, NY: Argus, 1895–1906.

Legislature. *New York in the War of the Rebellion.* 6 vols. 3rd ed. Albany, NY: Lyon, 1912.

North Carolina

Division of Archives and History. *North Carolina Troops, 1861–1865: A Roster.* 13 vols. Raleigh, NC: University of Graphics, 1993.

Ohio

The General Assembly; The Roster Commission. *Official Roster of the Soldiers of the State of Ohio.* 11 vols. Cincinnati, OH: Wilstach, Baldwin, 1886.

Oklahoma

Index to Applications for Pensions from the State of Oklahoma . . . Confederate.

Pennsylvania
Legislature (Bates). *History of Pennsylvania Volunteers, 1861–65.* 5 vols. Harrisburg, PA: State Printer, 1870.

Rhode Island
Adjutant General. *Register of Rhode Island Volunteers, 1861–1865.* 2 vols. Providence, RI: Freeman & Son, 1893.

South Carolina
South Carolina Troops in Confederate Service. 3 vols.

Tennessee
Centennial Civil War Commission of Tennessee. *Tennesseans in the Civil War, Parts I and II.*
Adjutant General. *Report of the Adjutant General of the State of Tennessee, 1861–1866.* Adjutant General's Office.
Military Annals of Tennessee, Confederate.
Index to Tennessee Confederate Pension Applications.
1890 Civil War Veterans Census: Tennessee.

Texas
Index to Texas CSA Pension Files.
1890 Civil War Veterans Census of Tennesseans in Texas.

Vermont
General Assembly. *Revised Roster of Vermont Volunteers and Lists of Vermonters Who Served in the Army and Navy of the United States during the War of the Rebellion, 1861–66.* Montpelier, VT: Watchman, 1892.

Virginia
The Virginia Regimental Histories Series. 45 vols. Lynchburg VA: Howard, 1987.
Guide to Virginia Military Organizations, 1861–1865.

West Virginia
Adjutant General, State of West Virginia. *Annual Report for the Year Ended December 31, 1864.* 1 vol. Charleston, WV: John M. Dermot, Public Printer, 1865.
Confederate Soldiers of Western Virginia.

Hardesty's West Virginia Counties. 8 vols. Richwood, WV: Jim Comstock, 1973

Lang, Theodore F. *Loyal West Virginia from 1861 to 1865.* Baltimore, MD: Deutsch Printing Company, 1895.

The Roster of Union Soldiers, 1861–1865, Volume 4. Wilmington, NC: Broadfoot Publishing, 1999.

Wisconsin

Adjutant General. *Roster of Wisconsin Volunteers, War of the Rebellion, 1861–1865.* 2 vols. Madison, WI: Democrat Printing Company, 1886.

WEBSITES
Civil War Navies

www.wtj.com/archives/acwnavies
www.csnavy.org/
www.tarleton.edu/~kjones/navy.html

General Sites Covering Multiple States
The following websites have listings for numerous regiments and units (some include navy and marine information). In addition to the websites discussed earlier in the this guide, such as the National Park Service's *Civil War Soldiers and Sailors Database* and the Civil War Center at Louisiana State University, the sites listed below should provide a wealth of information. If you have trouble finding a specific website, just go to *www.google.com* and enter your query, such as Civil War Roster South Carolina Database, and start looking through the search results. In addition to the website you were looking for, you should find others of equal interest.

www.cyndislist.com/cw.htm This is a fantastic site listing thousands of websites that have been grouped and categorized to make locating and searching them simple and rewarding.

www.geocities.com/SoHo/9787/index.html Among many other things, this site includes rosters and military records arranged by state.

www.carolyar.com/cwconfed.htm Lists names of Confederate soldiers from fifteen states, along with other information.

www.geocities.com/Area51/Lair/3680/cw/cw.html This is an unbelievable site. There are rosters for every state, along with some very unusual ones, such as units with American Indians, the Italian Regiment, the French Guard, and so on. This site is still growing. and in time, it probably will have every roster the webmaster can locate.

suvcw.org/mollus.htm Website for the Military Order of the Loyal Legion of the United States.

Alabama
www.rootsweb.com/~alcwroot/

Arizona
members.tripod.com/~azrebel/index.html

Arkansas
www.couchgenweb.com/civilwar/

Illinois
www.cyberdriveillinois.com/departments/archives/datcivil.html
illinoiscivilwar.org/

Indiana
www.accessgenealogy.com/military/civilwar/indiana/regiments.html

Iowa
iowa-counties.com/civilwar/

Maine
www.isn.net/~dhunter/mainem.html#top A database of Canadians who
served in Maine military units during the Civil War.

New York
www.sunsite.utk.edu/civil-war/unit2.html

Ohio
www.rbhayes.org/databases/soldiers/Index/Alpha/a.htm A Civil War
database containing soldiers indexed alphabetically. Includes such information as name, age, regiment, company, rank, and disposition.
www.ohiocivilwar.com/

Pennsylvania
pacivilwar.com
www.geocities.com/Heartland/Hills/3916/cwpa/

Texas
gen.1starnet.com/civilwar/texmain.htm

Virginia
www.iath.virginia.edu/vshadow/rostersearch.html

West Virginia
www.shepherd.wvnet.edu/gtmcweb/cwdbase.htm

Appendix E

Chronology of Battles

Date of Battle	Name and Location of Battle

Appendix F

Chart of Regiment's Organization

Name of Regiment _____   Head of Regiment _____

Company	Captain	Town of Origin
A		
B		
C		
D		
E		
F		
G		
H		
I		
K		

Appendix G

Command Structure

_____
Date

_____   _____
Corps   Commanding Officer

_____   _____
Division   Commanding Officer

_____   _____
Brigade   Commanding Officer

_____   _____

_____   _____

_____   _____

_____   _____

_____   _____

_____   _____
Regiments in Brigade   Commanding Officers

Appendix H

State Archives, Historical and Genealogical Societies

ALABAMA
Alabama Department of Archives and
    History
624 Washington Avenue
Montgomery, AL 36130-0100
(334) 242-4435
www.archives.state.al.us

Alabama Genealogy Society
Samford University Library
Harwell Goodwin Davis Library
Special Collection Department
800 Lake Shore Drive
Birmingham, AL 35229
(205) 870-2749
www.rootsweb.com/roots-l/USA/al.html

ARKANSAS
Arkansas Historical Commission and
    State Archives
One Capitol Mall
Little Rock, AR 72201
(501) 682-6900
www.ark-ives.com

Arkansas Genealogical Society
P.O. Box 908
Hot Springs, AR 71902-0908
(501) 262-4513
www.aagsnc.org/library/histsoc.html

Arkansas State Library
One Capital Mall, 5th Floor
Little Rock, AR 72201
(501) 682-1527
www.asl.lib.ar.us

CALIFORNIA
California State Archives
Division of Secretary of State's Office
1020 O Street
Sacramento, CA 95814
(916) 653-7715
www.ss.ca.gov/archives/archives.htm

California Genealogy Society
300 Brannan Street
P.O. Box 77105
San Francisco, CA 94107-0105
(415) 777-9936
members.tripod.com/~anamathis/index
    -5.html

California Historical Society
678 Mission Street
San Francisco, CA 94105
(415) 357-1848
www.calhist.org

California State Library
914 Capitol Mall
P.O. Box 942837
Sacramento, CA 94237
(916) 654-0183
www.library.ca.gov

COLORADO
Colorado State Archives
Division of Archives and Public
    Records
1313 Sherman Street
Room 1B-20
Denver, CO 80203
(303) 866-2358
www.archives.state.co.us/index.html

Colorado Genealogical Society
Denver Public Library
Genealogy Division
P.O. Box 9218
Denver, CO 80209-0218
(303) 571-1535
www.rootsweb.com/~cocgs/

Colorado Historical Society
1300 Broadway
Denver, CO 80203
(303) 866-2305
www.coloradohistory.org

Colorado State Library
201 East Colfax Avenue
Room 309
Denver, CO 80203
(303) 866-6900
www.cde.state.co.us/index_library
    .htm

CONNECTICUT
Connecticut State Archives
History and Genealogy Unit
231 Capitol Avenue
Hartford, CT 06106
(860) 757-6595
www.cslib.org/archives.htm

Connecticut State Library
231 Capitol Avenue
Hartford, CT 06106
(860) 757-6500
www.cslib.org

Connecticut Historical Society
One Elizabeth Street
Hartford, CT 06105
(860) 236-5621
www.chs.org

Connecticut Society of Genealo-
    gists
175 Maple Street, East Hartford
P.O. Box 435
Glastonbury, CT 06083-0435
(203) 569-0002
www.csginc.org

The Stamford Historical Society
1508 High Ridge Road
Stamford, CT 06903
(203) 329-1183
www.stamfordhistory.org

Connecticut Adjutant General
Records Office, State Attorney
360 Broad Street
Hartford, CT 06115
(860) 524-4953

DELAWARE
Division of Historical and Cultural
    Affairs
Hall of Records
121 Duke of York Street
Dover, DE 19901
(302) 739-5318
www.state.de.us/sos/dpa/

Delaware Genealogy Society
505 Market Street
Wilmington, DE 19801
(302) 655-7161
delgensoc.org

Historical Society of Delaware
505 Market Street
Wilmington, DE 19801
(302) 655-7161
www.hsd.org

Delaware State Library
43 South Dupont Highway
Dover, DE 19901
(302) 739-4748
www.state.lib.de.us/

FLORIDA
Florida State Archives
Bureau of Archives and Records
    Management
Division of Library and Information
    Services
Public Services Section
R. A. Gray Building
500 South Bronough Street
Tallahassee, FL 32399-0250
(850) 245-6700
www.dos.state.fl.us/dlis/barm/fsa
    .html

Florida Genealogy Society
P.O. Box 18624
Tampa, FL 33679-8624

Florida State Genealogy Society
P.O. Box 102496
Tallahassee, FL 32302-2249
(305) 375-5580
www.rootsweb.com/~flsgs/

Florida State Library
R. A. Gray Building
500 South Bronough Street
Tallahassee, FL 32399-0250
(850) 487-2651
dlis.dos.state.fl.us/stlib

GEORGIA
Georgia Department of Archives
    and History
330 Capitol Avenue, SE
Atlanta, GA 30334
(404) 656-2393
www.sos.state.ga.us/archives/

Georgia Genealogical Society
P.O. Box 54575
Atlanta, GA 30308-0575
(404) 475-4404
www.gagensociety.org

ILLINOIS
Illinois State Archives Division
Office of the Secretary of State
Archives Building
Capitol Complex
Springfield, IL 62756
(217) 782-3556
www.cyberdriveillinois.com/depart
    ments/archives/datcivil.html

Illinois State Genealogy Society
P.O. Box 10195
Springfield, IL 62791
(217) 789-1968
www.rootsweb.com/~ilsgs

Chicago Genealogical Society
P.O. Box 1160
Chicago, IL 60690
(773) 725-1306
www.chgogs.org

Illinois State Historical Society
210¹/₂ South 6th Street
Suite 200
Springfield, IL 62701
(217) 785-2781
www.prairenet.org/ishs

Illinois State Historical Library
Old State Capitol Building
Springfield, IL 62701
(217) 524-6358
www.state.il.us/hpa/lib

Illinois State Library
300 South 2nd Street
Springfield, IL 62701
(217) 785-5600
www.cyberdriveillinois.com/library/
    isl/isl.html

INDIANA
Indiana State Archives
117 State Library Building
Indianapolis, IN 46204
(317) 232-3660
www.state.in.us/icpr/webfile/
    archives/homepage.html

Indiana State Library
140 North Senate Avenue
Indianapolis, IN 46204
(317) 232-3689
www.statelib.lib.in.us

Indiana Genealogical Society
P.O. Box 10507
Fort Wayne, IN 46852-0507
www.indgensoc.org

Indiana Historical Society
450 West Ohio Street
Indianapolis, IN 46202-3269
(317) 232-1882
www.indianahistory.org

IOWA
An interesting and useful book,
    *Discovering Your Iowa Civil
    War Ancestry* (60 pages, 1993),
    can be ordered from Meyer Pub-
    lishing, Box 247, Garrison, IA
    52229, (800) 477-5046. The cost
    is (or was) $8.00.

State Historical Society of Iowa and
    Iowa State Archives
Capitol Complex
600 East Locust
Des Moines, IA 50319-0290
(515) 281-5111
www.culturalaffairs.org

Iowa Genealogical Society
6000 Douglas
P.O. Box 7735
Des Moines, IA 50322-7735
(515) 276-0287
www.iowagenealogy.org

Iowa State Library
East 12th and Grand
Des Moines, IA 50319
(515) 281-4105
www.silo.lib.ia.us

KANSAS
Kansas State Historical Society
Reference Section
Kansas History Center
6425 SW Sixth Avenue
Topeka, KS 66615-1099
(785) 272-8681
www.kshs.org

Kansas Genealogical Research
  Society
700 Avenue G at Vine Street
P.O. Box 103
Dodge City, KS 67801
(316) 225-1951

Kansas State Library
State Capitol Building
300 SW 10th Avenue, Room 343-N
Topeka, KS 66612
(785) 296-3296 or (800) 432-3919
skyways.lib.ks.us/kansas/KSL/

KENTUCKY
Kentucky State Archives
Public Records Division
300 Coffee Tree Road, 1st Floor
P.O. Box 537
Frankfort, KY 40602-0537
(502) 564-8300 or 8704
www.kdla.state.ky.us/

Kentucky Genealogical Society
P.O. Box 153
Frankfort, KY 40602
(502) 223-0492
www.kygs.org

Kentucky Historical Society
P.O. Box H
Frankfort, KY 40602
(502) 564-1792
www.kentuckyhistory.org

LOUISIANA
Office of the Secretary of the State
Louisiana State Archives
3851 Essen Lane
P.O. Box 94125
Baton Rouge, LA 70809-2137
(225) 922-1000
www.sec.state.la.us/archives/
  archives/archives-index.htm

Louisiana Genealogical and Historical Society
P.O. Box 82060
Baton Rouge, LA 70884-2060
(225) 766-3018
www.rootsweb.com/~la-lghs/

Louisiana State Library
701 North 4th Street
Baton Rouge, LA 70821
(225) 342-4913
www.state.lib.la.us/

MAINE
Maine State Archives
State House Station #84
Augusta, ME 04333-0084
(207) 287-5795
www.state.me.us/sos/arc/general/
  admin/arcserv.htm

Maine Genealogical Society
P.O. Box 221
Farmington, ME 04938-0221
www.rootsweb.com/~megs/Maine
  GS.htm

Maine Historical Society
485 Congress Street
Portland, ME 04101
(207) 774-1822
www.mainehistory.com

Pejepscot Historical Society
159 Park Row
Brunswick, ME 04011
(207) 729-6606
www.curtislibrary.com/pejepscot.htm

MARYLAND
Maryland State Archives
Hall of Records Building
350 Rowe Boulevard
Annapolis, MD 21401
(410) 260-6400 or (800) 235-4045
www.mdarchives.state.md.us/

Maryland Genealogical Society
201 West Monument Street
Baltimore, MD 21201
(410) 685-3750
www.rootsweb.com/~mdsgs/

MASSACHUSETTS
Massachusetts Archives Division
  of the Commonwealth
220 Morrisey Boulevard
Boston, MA 02125
(617) 727-2816
www.magnet.state.ma.us/sec/arc/
  arcidx.htm

New England Historic Genealogical
  Society
101 Newbury Street
Boston, MA 02116
(617) 536-5740
www.nehgs.org

Massachusetts Historical Society
1154 Boylston Street
Boston, MA 02215
(617) 536-1608
masshist.org

MICHIGAN
State Archives
Michigan Historical Society
Department of State
717 West Allegan Street
Lansing, MI 48918
(517) 373-1408
www.sos.state.mi.us/history/archive/
  archive.html

Michigan Genealogical Council
P.O. Box 80953
Lansing, MI 48908-0953
www.rootsweb.com/~mimgc/

Michigan Department of State
Michigan History Division
State Archives Unit
3405 North Logan Street
Lansing, MI 48906

MINNESOTA
Minnesota Historical Society
Research Center
345 West Kellogg Boulevard
St. Paul, MN 55102
(651) 296-6126
www.mnhs.org/

Minnesota Genealogical Society
5768 Olson Memorial Highway
Golden Valley, MN 55422
(763) 595-9347
www.mtn.org/mgs/

MISSISSIPPI

If you are researching someone
from Mississippi, you may want
to obtain a copy of *Tracing Your
Mississippi Ancestors* from the
University of Mississippi, (800)
737-7788. This is a source book
for genealogical research, with
numerous sources for records
and information in Mississippi.
The cost of the book is (or was)
$33.00.

Mississippi Department of Archives
and History
P.O. Box 571
Jackson, MS 39205-0571
(601) 359-6850
www.mdah.state.ms.us

Historical and Genealogical Association of Mississippi
618 Avalon Road
Jackson, MS 39206
(601) 362-3079

Mississippi Genealogical Society
P.O. Box 5301
Jackson, MS 39296-5301
members.tripod.com/smsghs

MISSOURI

Missouri State Archives
State Information Center
P.O. Box 778
Jefferson City, MO 65101
(573) 751-3280
mosl.sos.state.mo.us/
   rec-man/arch.html

Missouri State Genealogical
   Association
P.O. Box 833
Columbia, MO 65205-0833
(816) 747-9330
www.mosga.org

Heart of America Genealogical
   Society
c/o Public Library
311 East 12th Street
Kansas City, MO 64106

Missouri Historical Society and
   Archives
Jefferson Memorial Building
Forest Park, P.O. Box 11940
St. Louis, MO 63112
(314) 746-4500
mohistory.org

State of Missouri
Office of the Adjutant General
2302 Militia Drive
Jefferson City, MO 65101
(314) 526-9500

MONTANA
Montana Historical Society
Division of Archives and Manu-
    scripts
Memorial Building
P.O. Box 201201
225 North Roberts Street
Helena, MT 59620
(406) 444-2694
www.his.state.mt.us/

Montana State Genealogical Society
P.O. Box 555
Chester, MT 59522
www.rootsweb.com/~mtmsgs/

Montana State Library
1515 East 6th Street
P.O. Box 201800
Helena, MT 59620
(406) 444-3115
www.msl.state.mt.us

NEW HAMPSHIRE
New Hampshire Division of
    Records Management and
    Archives
71 South Fruit Street
Concord, NH 03301-2410
(603) 271-2236
www.state.nh.us/state

New Hampshire Historical Society
The Tuck Library
30 Park Street
Concord, NH 03301-6394
(603) 225-3381
www.nhhistory.org

NEW JERSEY
New Jersey State Archives
Division of Archives and Records
    Management
State Library Building
225 West State Street, Level 2
Trenton, NJ 08625-0307
(609) 292-6260
www.state.nj.us/state/darm/links/
    archives.html

Genealogical Society of New Jersey
P.O. Box 1291
New Brunswick, NJ 08903
www.rootsweb.com/~njgsnj/main
    .htm

New Jersey Historical Society
52 Park Place
Newark, NJ 07102
(973) 596-8500
www.jerseyhistory.org

NEW YORK
New York Historical Society
2 West 77th Street at Central Park
    West
New York, NY 10024
(212) 873-3400
www.nyhistory.org

New York State Archives and
    Records Administration
New York Department of Education
Cultural Education Center #11D40
Albany, NY 12230
(518) 474-8955
www.sara.nysed.gov

New York Genealogical and
   Biographical Society
122 East 58th Street
New York, NY 10022-1939
(212) 755-8532
www.nygbs.org

Central New York Genealogical
   Society
P.O. Box 104
Covin Station
Syracuse, NY 13205
www.rootsweb.com/~nycnygs/

NORTH CAROLINA
North Carolina Department of
   Cultural Resources
Division of Archives and History
4614 Mail Service Center
Raleigh, NC 27699-4614
(919) 733-3952
(The above is the mailing address;
   the Division of Archives and
   History is located at 109 East
   Jones Street in Raleigh.)
www.ah.dcr.state.nc.us/sections/
   archives/arch/

North Carolina Genealogical
   Society
P.O. Box 1492
Raleigh, NC 27602
(919) 733-3991
www.ncgenealogy.org

State Library of North Carolina
State Library Building
109 East Jones Street
Raleigh, NC 27601
(919) 733-3270
statelibrary.dcr.state.nc.us/
   ncslhome.htm

OHIO
State Library of Ohio
65 South Front Street, Room 510
Columbus, OH 43266-0334
(614) 644-6966
winslo.state.oh.us

Ohio Historical Society
1982 Velma Avenue
Columbus, OH 43211-2497
(614) 297-2525 or 2300
www.ohiohistory.org/

The Ohio Genealogical Society
34 Sturges Avenue
P.O. Box 2625
Mansfield, OH 44906
(419) 522-9077
www.ogs.org

Ohio State Archives
1985 Velma Avenue
Columbus, OH 43211
(614) 466-1500
www.ohiohistory.org/resource/
   statearc

OKLAHOMA
Oklahoma Department of Libraries
Historical Building
200 NE 18th Street
Oklahoma City, OK 73105
(800) 522-8116, ext. 209
www.odl.state.ok.us/oar/index2.htm

Oklahoma Historical Society
2100 North Lincoln Boulevard
Oklahoma City, OK 73105
(405) 521-2491
www.ok-history.mus.ok.us

Oklahoma Genealogical Society
P.O. Box 12986
Oklahoma City, OK 73157-2986
www.rootsweb.com/~okgs/

PENNSYLVANIA
Pennsylvania State Archives
Reference Section
350 North Street
Harrisburg, PA 17120-0090
(717) 783-3281
www.phmc.state.pa.us/DAM/psa.htm

Historical Society of Pennsylvania
1300 Locust Street
Philadelphia, PA 19107-5699
(215) 732-6200
www.hsp.org

Camp Curtin Historical Society
2221 North 6th Street
Harrisburg, PA 17110
www.campcurtin.org

Northeast Pennsylvania Genealogical Society
P.O. Box 1776
Shavertown, PA 18708-0776
www.rootsweb.com/~panepgs/

State Library of Pennsylvania
Walnut Street and Commonwealth
   Avenue
P.O. Box 1601
Harrisburg, PA 17105
(717) 783-5950
www.statelibrary.state.pa.us

RHODE ISLAND
Rhode Island State Archives
Department of Archives and
   History
337 Westminster Street
Providence, RI 02903-3302
(401) 222-2353
www.state.ri.us/archives/

Rhode Island Genealogical Society
P.O. Box 433
Greenville, RI 02828
users.ids.net/~ricon/rigs.html

Rhode Island State Historical
   Society
121 Hope Street
Providence, RI 02906
(401) 331-8575
www.rihs.org

SOUTH CAROLINA
The Guide to Civil War Records: A
   Guide to the South Carolina
   Department of Archives and His-
   tory, by Patrick McCawley, can
   be ordered from the South Caro-
   lina Department of Archives and
   History, P.O. Box 11669,
   Columbia, SC 29211. The cost is
   (or was) $5.00 plus shipping.

South Carolina Department of
   Archives and History
8301 Parklane Road
Columbia, SC 29223
(803) 896-6100
www.state.sc.us/scdah/homepage
   .htm

South Carolina Historical Society
100 Meeting Street
Charleston, SC 29401
(843) 723-3225
www.schistory.org

South Carolina Genealogical Society
P.O. Box 492
Columbia, SC 29202
www.scgen.org

South Carolina State Library
1500 Senate Street
P.O. Box 11469
Columbia, SC 29211
(803) 734-8666
www.state.sc.us/scsl

TENNESSEE
Tennessee State Library and
    Archives
State Library and Archives Building
403 7th Avenue North
Nashville, TN 37243-0312
(615) 741-2764
www.state.tn.us/sos/statelib/
    tslahome.htm

The Tennessee Genealogical
    Society
9114 Davies Plantation Road
Brunswick, TN 38014
(901) 381-1447
www.rootsweb.com/~tngs/

TEXAS
Texas State Library and Archives
    Commission
1201 Brazos Street
Box 12927, Capitol Station
Austin, TX 78711-2927
(512) 463-5463
www.tsl.state.tx.us/lobby/arcfirst.htm

Texas State Genealogical Society
2507 Tannehill
Houston, TX 77008-3052
(713) 864-6862
www.rootsweb.com/~txsgs/

VERMONT
Vermont State Archives
Office of the Secretary of State
Redstone Building
26 Terrace Street
Montpelier, VT 05609-1101
(802) 828-2363
vermont-archives.org

Vermont Historical Society Library
    and Museum
Pavilion Building
109 State Street
Montpelier, VT 05602-0901
(802) 828-2291
www.state.vt.us/vhs

Genealogical Society of Vermont
P.O. Box 1553
St. Albans, VT 05478-1006
www.rootsweb.com/~vtgsv

Vermont Department of Libraries
109 State Street
Montpelier, VT 05609-0901
(802) 828-3261
www.uvm.edu/~histpres/vtiana/
   vtlib.html

VIRGINIA
Library of Virginia
Archives Division
800 East Broad Street
Richmond, VA 23219
(804) 692-3500
www.lva.lib.va.us/

Virginia Genealogical Society
5001 West Broad Street, Suite 115
Richmond, VA 23230-3023
(804) 285-8954
www.vgs.org

Virginia Historical Society
428 North Boulevard
Richmond, VA 23220
(804) 358-4901
www.vahistorical.org

Sergeant Kirkland's Museum and
   Historical Society, Inc.
912 Lafayette Boulevard
Fredericksburg, VA 22401
(540) 899-5565
www.kirklands.org

WEST VIRGINIA
West Virginia State Archives
Archives and History Library
1900 Kanawha Boulevard, East
Charleston, WV 25305-0300
(304) 558-0230, ext. 168
www.wvculture.org/history/
   wvsamenu.html

Division of Archives and History
West Virginia Library Commission
Department of Culture and History
Science and Cultural Center
Capitol Complex
Charleston, WV 25305
(304) 558-0220
www.wvculture.org/history/
   wvah.html

West Virginia Genealogical Society
P.O. Box 249
Elkview, WV 25071
www.rootsweb.com/~wvgs

West Virginia Historical Society
Cultural Center
1900 Kanawha Boulevard East
Charleston, WV 25305-0300
(304) 558-0220
www.wvculture.org/history/
   guide2.html

WISCONSIN

An excellent book for researching someone from Wisconsin
is *Researching Your Civil War
Ancestors in Wisconsin*. This
258-page book can be
ordered from Bivouac Publications, 1232 Arlington
Avenue, Manitowoc, WI
54220, (414) 682-0235. The
cost is (or was) $16.00.

State Historical Society of
Wisconsin
816 State Street
Madison, WI 53706
(608) 264-6400
www.shsw.wisc.edu/index.html

Wisconsin State Genealogical
Society
2109 20th Avenue
Monroe, WI 53566
(608) 325-2609
www.rootsweb.com/~wsgs

Appendix I

National Historic Sites and Battlefield Parks

Andersonville — Andersonville National Historic Site
496 Cemetery Road
Andersonville, GA 31711
(229) 924-0343
www.nps.gov/ande/

Antietam (Sharpsburg) — Antietam National Battlefield
P.O. Box 158
Sharpsburg, MD 21782-0158
(301) 432-5124
www.nps.gov/anti/

Appomattox Court House — Appomattox Court House National Historic
Park
Highway 24, P.O. Box 218
Appomattox, VA 24522
(434) 352-8987
www.nps.gov/apco/

Brices Cross Roads — Brices Cross Roads National Battlefield Site
2680 Natchez Trace Parkway
Tupelo, MS 38804
(662) 680-4025 or (800) 305-7417
www.nps.gov/brcr/

Chancellorsville — See Fredericksburg & Spotsylvania National Military
Park

Chattanooga — Chickamauga & Chattanooga National Military Park
P.O. Box 2128
Fort Oglethorpe, GA 30742
(706) 866-9241
www.nps.gov/chch/

Chickamauga — See Chickamauga & Chattanooga National Military
Park

Cold Harbor — See Richmond National Battlefield Park

Cumberland Gap — Cumberland Gap National Historical Park
U.S. 25E South
P.O. Box 1848
Middlesboro, KY 40965-1848
(606) 248-2817
www.nps.gov/cuga/

Drewry's Bluff — See Richmond National Battlefield Park

Fort Donelson — Fort Donelson National Battlefield
P.O. Box 434
Dover, TN 37058-0434
(931) 232-5706
www.nps.gov/fodo/

Fort Gilmer — See Richmond National Battlefield Park

Fort Harrison — See Richmond National Battlefield Park

Fort McHenry — Fort McHenry National Monument and Historic Shrine
End of East Fort Avenue
Baltimore, MD 21230-5393
(410) 962-4290
www.nps.gov/fomc/

Fort Moultrie — Fort Moultrie National Monument
1214 Middle Street
Sullivan's Island, SC 29482
(843) 883-3123
www.nps.gov/fomo/

Fort Pulaski — Fort Pulaski National Monument
P.O. Box 30757
Savannah, GA 31410-0757
(912) 786-5787
www.nps.gov/fopu/

Fort Scott — Fort Scott National Historic Site
P.O. Box 918
Fort Scott, KS 66701-0918
(620) 223-0310
www.nps.gov/fosc/

Fort Sumter — Fort Sumter National Monument
1214 Middle Street
Sullivan's Island, SC 29482
(843) 883-3123
www.nps.gov/fosu/

Fredericksburg — Fredericksburg & Spotsylvania National Military Park
The Chatham House
120 Chatham Lane
Fredericksburg, VA 22405-2508
(540) 371-0802, (540) 373-6122, or (540) 786-2880
www.nps.gov/frsp/

Gaines' Mill — See Richmond National Battlefield Park

Gettysburg — Gettysburg National Military Park
97 Taneytown Road
Gettysburg, PA 17325-2804
(717) 334-1124
www.nps.gov/gett/

Harpers Ferry — Harpers Ferry National Historical Park
P.O. Box 65
Harpers Ferry, WV 25425
(304) 535-6298
www.nps.gov/hafe/

Kennesaw Mountain — Kennesaw Mountain National Battlefield Park
900 Kennesaw Mountain Drive
Kennesaw, GA 30152
(770) 427-4686, ext. 0
www.nps.gov/kemo/

Malvern Hill — See Richmond National Battlefield Park

Manassas (Bull Run) — Manassas National Battlefield Park
12521 Lee Highway
Manassas, VA 20109-2005
(703) 361-1339
www.nps.gov/mana/

Miscellaneous Collections — U.S. Army Military History Institute
22 Ashburn Drive
Carlisle Barracks
Carlisle, PA 17013-5008
(717) 245-3611
www.carlisle.army.mil/usamhi/

Monocacy — Monocacy National Battlefield
4801 Urbana Pike
Frederick, MD 21704-7307
(301) 662-3515
www.nps.gov/mono/

Pea Ridge — Pea Ridge National Military Park
P.O. Box 700
Pea Ridge, AR 72751-0700
(501) 451-8122
www.nps.gov/peri/

Pecos (Glorieta) — Pecos National Historical Park
P.O. Box 418
Pecos, NM 87552-0418
(505) 757-6414, ext. 1
www.nps.gov/peco/

Petersburg — Petersburg National Battlefield
1539 Hickory Hill Road
Petersburg, VA 2303-4721
(804) 732-3531
www.nps.gov/pete/

Richmond — Richmond National Battlefield Park
3215 East Broad Street
Richmond, VA 23223
(804) 226-1981
www.nps.gov/rich/

Rock Creek — Rock Creek Park
3545 Williamburg Lane, NW
Washington, DC 20008
(202) 426-6828
www.nps.gov/rocr

Shiloh (Pittsburg Landing) — Shiloh National Military Park
1055 Pittsburg Landing Road
Shiloh, TN 38376
(731) 689-5696
www.nps.gov/shil/

Spotsylvania Court House — See Fredericksburg & Spotsylvania
National Military Park

Stones River — Stones River National Battlefield
3501 Old Nashville Highway
Murfreesboro, TN 37129
(615) 893-9501
www.nps.gov/stri/

Tupelo — Tupelo National Battlefield
2680 Natchez Trace Parkway
Tupelo, MS 38804
(800) 305-7417
www.nps.gov/tupe/

Vicksburg — Vicksburg National Military Park
3201 Clay Street
Vicksburg, MS 39183
(601) 636-0583
www.nps.gov/vick/

Wilderness — See Fredericksburg & Spotsylvania National Military Park

Wilson's Creek — Wilson's Creek National Battlefield
6424 West Farm Road 182
Republic, MO 65738-9514
(417) 732-2662
www.nps.gov/wicr/

Yorktown — Colonial National Historic Park
Route 17 and Goosley Road
Yorktown, VA 23690
(757) 898-2410
www.nps.gov/colo/

Appendix J

Confederate Pension and Military Records

CONFEDERATE PENSION RECORDS

At various times after the end of the Civil War, the individual states formerly constituting the Confederacy provided pensions for many of the men who had served for the South. A person could apply for a pension from the state where he lived, even though he actually had served in a unit from another state. Various restrictions were placed on the granting of pensions, with some states requiring that the applicant be disabled due to his service in the war or be indigent.

The addresses, telephone numbers, and website addresses for the various state archives listed below are provided in Appendix H. In addition to the websites for those archives, try websites that have links to other websites with pension information, such as *www.cyndislist.com/cw.htm*. An excellent collection of materials on Confederate pension records is available through the National Archives website, *www.archives.gov/research_room/ genealogy/military/confederate_pension_records.com*. In fact, much of the information for the following description of Confederate pension records comes from that website.

Alabama

Alabama Department of Archives and History (see Appendix H).

Alabama first began granting pensions in 1867, with subsequent revisions to its pension program in 1886 and 1891. Initially, pensions were granted only to men who had lost an arm or leg during the war. Later the state granted pensions to veterans' widows and to the indigent.

Arkansas

Arkansas Historical Commission and State Archives (see Appendix H).

Arkansas first began granting pensions in 1891. Initially, pensions were granted only to indigent veterans. Later, in 1915, this was modified to also provide pensions for veterans' widows and mothers. There are two published listings for Arkansas pension applications: Desmond Walls Allen, *Index to Confederate Pension Applications* (Conway, AR: Arkansas Research, 1991); and Francis Terry Ingmire, *Arkansas Confederate Veterans and Widows Pensions Applications* (St. Louis: F. T. Ingmire, 1985).

Florida
Florida State Archives (see Appendix H).

The state of Florida began granting pensions to veterans in 1885 and extended this to veterans' widows in 1889. For a published listing of these applications and pension numbers, see Virgil White, *Register of Florida CSA Pension Applications* (Waynesboro, TN: National Historical Publishing Co., 1989).

The pensions also can be searched on-line from the Florida State Archives webpage, *dlis.dos.state.fl.us/barm/PensionFiles.html.*

Georgia
Georgia Department of Archives and History (see Appendix H).

The state of Georgia began granting pensions in 1870 and expanded its program in 1879 and 1894. Initially, these were limited to veterans who were disabled. Later it included veterans and their widows who were in financial need due to poverty and old age. For a published listing of these applications, see Virgil White, *Index to Georgia Civil War Confederate Pension Files* (Waynesboro, TN: National Historical Publishing Co., 1989).

Although it is not the easiest website to navigate, Georgia State University has the index for Georgia pension applications on-line at *docuweb.gsu.edu/scripts/webmain.dll?Anonymous.*

Kentucky
Kentucky State Archives (see Appendix H).

Kentucky did not begin granting pensions to Confederate veterans or their widows until 1912, more than forty-five years after the war had ended. For a published index of these applications, see Alicia Simpson, *Index of Confederate Pension Applications, Commonwealth of Kentucky* (Frankfort, KY: Division of Archives and Records Management, Department of Library and Archives, 1978).

Louisiana
Louisiana State Archives (see Appendix H).

Louisiana first began granting pensions to indigent veterans and their widows in 1898.

Mississippi
Mississippi Department of Archives and History (see Appendix H).

Mississippi first began granting pensions to indigent veterans and their widows in 1888. For a published index of these applications, see Betty C. Wilshire, *Mississippi Confederate Pension Applications* (Carrollton, MS: Pioneer Publishing Co., 1994).

Missouri
Missouri State Archives (see Appendix H).

In 1911, Missouri began granting pensions to indigent veterans. Unlike most states, it did not grant pensions to veterans' widows. In addition, Missouri maintained a home for disabled veterans. Both the pension applications and the veterans' home applications are on file in the archives.

North Carolina
North Carolina Department of Cultural Resources (see Appendix H).

Two years after the war, in 1867, North Carolina began granting pensions to veterans who had been blinded or lost a limb during the war. In 1885, this was extended to cover all disabled indigent veterans and their widows.

Oklahoma
Oklahoma Department of Libraries, Archives and Records Management Division (see Appendix H).

The last state to grant pensions to Confederate veterans and their widows, Oklahoma began granting pensions in 1915. For a published index of the pension applications, see Oklahoma Genealogical Society, *Index to Applications for Pensions from the State of Oklahoma Submitted by Confederate Soldiers, Sailors and Their Widows* (Oklahoma City: Genealogical Society Projects Committee, 1969).

South Carolina
South Carolina Department of Archives and History (see Appendix H).

In 1887, South Carolina began granting pensions to veterans and widows in financial need. Beginning in 1889, the South Carolina comptroller started including a listing of the veterans receiving pensions in his Annual Report. In 1919, the law was expanded to provide pensions to veterans and widows regardless of financial need. For applications submitted between 1887 and 1919, you will need to research the comptroller's *Annual Reports* to identify the year your ancestor submitted an application. You may then be able to obtain a copy of the application, but unfortunately, it seems that most of the applications prior to 1919 are no longer in existence. Pension applications from 1919 and later are fairly complete and are arranged in alphabetical order. In addition to pension applications, the archives contain Confederate Home applications and inmate records for veterans.

Some pension records can be found at the following websites: *www.ccpl.org/scr.html* and *www.state.sc.us/scdah/genealre.htm.*

Tennessee
Tennessee State Library and Archives (see Appendix H).

Tennessee began granting pensions to indigent veterans in 1891 and to veterans' widows in 1905. For a published index of these applications, see Samuel Sistler, *Index to Tennessee Confederate Pension Applications* (Nashville: Sistler & Associates, 1995).

In addition to pension applications, records pertaining to the Confederate veterans' home can be searched on-line at *www.state.tn.us/sos/ statelib/pubsvs/csh_intr.htm.*

Texas
Texas State Library and Archives Commission (see Appendix H).

In 1881, Texas took the unusual step of setting aside 1,280 acres for disabled Confederate veterans. A few years later, in 1889, Texas also began granting pensions to indigent veterans and their widows. For a published index of the applications, see Virgil D. White, *Index to Texas CSA Pension Files* (Waynesboro, TN: National Historical Publishing Co., 1989).

The pension applications can be searched on-line at *www.tsl.state.tx.us/ lobby/cpi/cpindex.htm.*

Virginia
Library of Virginia, Archives Division (see Appendix H).

Virginia began granting pensions to veterans and their widows in 1888. The index for these records can be searched on-line at *image.vtls.com/ collections/CW.html.*

CONFEDERATE MILITARY RECORDS
Some military records for Confederate soldiers can be found in the National Archives (see Chapter 7 on the National Archives.) For a collection of Confederate military records, see the website *198.17.62.51/collections/ cc_military.html#confederate.*

Appendix K

Regional Branches of the National Archives

ALASKA
NARA's Pacific Alaska Region
(Anchorage)
654 West 3rd Avenue
Anchorage, AK 99501-2145
(907) 271-2443
www.nara.gov/regional/anchorag.html

CALIFORNIA
NARA's Pacific Region (Laguna
Niguel)
24000 Avila Road
1st Floor, East Entrance
P.O. Box 6719
Laguna, CA 92607-6719
(949) 360-2641
www.nara.gov/regional/laguna.html

NARA's Pacific Region (San Francisco)
1000 Commodore Drive
San Bruno, CA 94066-2350
(650) 876-9001
www.nara.gov/regional/sanfranc.html

COLORADO
NARA's Rocky Mountain Region
Building 48, Denver Federal Center
West 6th Avenue and Kipling Street
Denver, CO 80225-0307
(303) 236-0817
www.nara.gov/regional/denver.html

GEORGIA
NARA's Southeast Region
1557 St. Joseph Avenue
East Point, GA 30344-2593
(404) 763-7474
www.nara.gov/regional/atlanta.html

ILLINOIS
NARA's Great Lakes Region
7358 South Pulaski Road
Chicago, IL 60629-5898
(773) 581-7816
www.nara.gov/regional/chicago.html

MARYLAND
Office of Regional Records Services
Administration
8601 Adelphi Road
College Park, MD 20740-6001
(301) 713-7200

Washington National Records
  Center
4205 Suitland Road
Suitland, MD 20746-8001
(301) 457-7000
www.nara.gov/records/wnrc.html

MASSACHUSETTS
NARA's Northeast Region (Boston)
380 Trapelo Road
Waltham, MA 02452-6399
(781) 647-8104
www.nara.gov/regional/boston.html

NARA's Northeast Region (Pittsfield)
10 Conte Drive
Pittsfield, MA 01201-8230
(413) 445-6885
www.nara.gov/regional/pittsfie.html

MISSOURI
NARA's Central Plains Region
  (Kansas City)
2312 East Bannister Road
Kansas City, MO 64131-3011
(816) 926-6982
www.nara.gov/regional/kansas.html

NARA's Central Plains Region
  (Lee's Summit)
200 Space Center Drive
Lee's Summit, MO 64064-1182
(816) 478-7089
www.nara.gov/regional/leesumit.html

NARA's National Personnel
  Records Center
Civilian Personnel Records
111 Winnebago Street
St. Louis, MO 63118-4199
(314) 538-5761
www.nara.gov/regional/cpr.html

NARA's National Personnel
  Records Center
Military Personnel Records
9700 Page Avenue
St. Louis, MO 63132-5100
(314) 538-5761
www.nara.gov/regional/mpr.html

NEW YORK
NARA's Northeast Region (New
  York City)
201 Varick Street
New York, NY 10014-4811
(212) 337-1300
www.nara.gov/regional/newyork
  .html

OHIO
NARA's Great Lakes Region
  (Dayton)
3150 Springboro Road
Dayton, OH 45439-1883
(937) 225-2852
www.nara.gov/regional/dayton.html

PENNSYLVANIA
NARA's Mid-Atlantic Region (Center City Philadelphia)
900 Market Street
Philadelphia, PA 19107-4292
(215) 597-3000
www.nara.gov/regional/philacc.html

NARA's Mid-Atlantic Region
  (Northeast Philadelphia)
14700 Townsend Road
Philadelphia, PA 19154-1096
(215) 671-9027
www.nara.gov/regional/philane.html

TEXAS
NARA's Southwest Region
501 West Felix Street, Building 1
Fort Worth, TX 76115-3405
(817) 334-5515
www.nara.gov/regional/ftworth.html

WASHINGTON
NARA's Pacific Alaska Region
  (Seattle)
6125 Sand Point Way, NE
Seattle, WA 98115-7999
(206) 526-6501
www.nara.gov/regional/seattle.html

Appendix L

Other Museums, Libraries, and Collections of Interest

University of Arkansas
Libraries, Special Collections
Fayetteville, AR 72701-1201
(501) 575-4101
cavern.uark.edu/libinfo/speccoll/
    civilwar1.html

Atlanta History Center
130 West Paces Ferry Road
Atlanta, GA 30305
(404) 814-4000
www.atlhist.org

Auburn University
Library, Special Collections and
    Archives
Civil War Archival Collections
231 Mell Street
Auburn, AL 36849-5606
(334) 844-1738
www.lib.auburn.edu/archive/find-
    aid/cwcover.htm

Boston Public Library
Rare Books and Manuscripts Division
700 Boylston Street
Copley Square
Boston, MA 02117
(617) 536-5400 ext. 2225
www.bpl.org/www/rb/rbd.htm

Bowling Green State University
Center for Archival Collections
Jerome Library, 5th Floor
Bowling Green, OH 43403
(419) 372-2411
www.bgsu.edu/colleges/library/cac/
    civilwar.html

Brown University
John Hay Library
Special Collections
20 Prospect Street, Box A
Providence, RI 02912
(401) 863-3723
www.brown.edu/Facilities/Univer-
    sity_Library/collections/manu-
    scripts/mss.html

Carroll College
Institute for Civil War Studies
McAllister Hall
100 North East Avenue
Waukesha, WI 53186
(262) 547-1211
carroll1.cc.edu/civilwar/

University of Chicago
Library, Department of Special Collections
1100 East 57th Street
Chicago, IL 60637
(773) 702-4685
www.lib.uchicago.edu/e/spcl/
civwar.html

Civil War Library and Museum
1805 Pine Street
Philadelphia, PA 19103
(215) 735-8156
www.netreach.net/~cwlm/

Confederate Museum
929 Camp Street
New Orleans, LA 70130
(504) 523-4522
www.confederatemuseum.com

Confederate Naval Museum
P.O. Box 1022
Columbus, GA 31902
(706) 327-9798
www.portcolumbus.org

Confederate States Navy Museum,
Library and Research Institute
P.O. Box 50950
Mobile, AL 36605-0950
www.csnavy.org/

University of Delaware
Library, Special Collections
Newark, DE 19717-5267
(302) 831-2229
www.lib.udel.edu/ud/spec/

Duke University
Rare Book, Manuscript and Special
Collections Library
Durham, NC 27708-0185
(919) 660-5822
odyssey.lib.duke.edu/

Emory University
Robert W. Woodruff Library
Special Collections and Archives
540 Asbury Circle
Atlanta, GA 30322
(404) 727-6887
info.library.emory.edu/Special/
guides-civilwar-pre.html

Florida State University
Library, Special Collections
www.fsu.edu/~speccoll/civildir.htm

Henry Huntington Library
1151 Oxford Road
San Marino, CA 91108
(626) 405-2141
www.huntington.org

Hill Junior College
Harold B. Simpson History
Complex
(formerly known as the Confederate Research Center at Hill
Junior College)
P.O. Box 619
Hillsboro, TX 76645
(254) 582-2555, ext. 242
www.hill-college.cc.tx.us/museum/
mainpage/research/research.html

The Library of Virginia
800 East Broad Street
Richmond, VA 23219-8000
(804) 692-3500
www.lva.lib.va.us/dlp/index.htm

Louisiana State University
The United States Civil War Center
Raphael Semmes Drive
Baton Rouge, LA 70803
(225) 578-3151
www.cwc.lsu.edu/

University of Michigan
William L. Clements Library
Manuscript Division
909 South University Avenue
Ann Arbor, MI 48109-1190
(734) 764-2347
www.clements.umich.edu/
    Manuscripts.html

Museum of the Confederacy
1201 Clay Street
Richmond, VA 23219-1615
(804) 649-1861
www.moc.org

Naval History Center
Washington Navy Yard
805 Kidder Breese, S.E.
Washington, DC 20374-5060
www.history.navy.mil/

New England Civil War Museum
Thomas J. O'Connell Library
14 Park Place
Vernon, CT 06066
pages.cthome.net/ne.civilwar.mus

New York Public Library
Manuscripts and Archives Division
5th Avenue and 42nd Street
Room 328
New York, NY 10018-2788
(212) 930-0801
www.nypl.org/research/chss/spe/
    rbk/mss.html

University of North Carolina
Manuscript Department
Campus Box 3926
Wilson Library
Chapel Hill, NC 27514
(919) 962-1345
www.lib.unc.edu/mss

Old Dominion University
The Perry Library
Hampton Boulevard
Norfolk, VA 23529
(757) 683-4154
www.lib.odu.edu/aboutlib/spccol/
    civilwar.shtml

Princeton University
Library, Manuscript Collections
Reference Librarian/Archivist
Princeton, NJ 08544
(609) 258-3174
www.princeton.edu/~pressman/
    history.htm

Shepherd College
George Tyler Moore Center for the
    Study of the Civil War
Shepherdstown, WV 25443
(304) 876-5429
www.shepherd.wvnet.edu/
    gtmcweb/cwcenter.htm

Soldiers & Sailors Memorial Hall
4141 5th Avenue
Pittsburgh, PA 15213
(412) 621-4253
www.soldiersandsailorshall.org

University of South Carolina
South Caroliniana Library
Manuscripts Division
Columbia, SC 29208
(803) 777-5183
www.sc.edu/library/socar/mscrpts/

University of Southern Mississippi
McCain Library and Archives
Civil War Collections
Box 5148
Hattiesburg, MS 39406-5148
(601) 266-4348
www.lib.usm.edu/~archives/subj-
   cw.htm

University of Tennessee
University Archives and Special
   Collections
Hoskins Library
Cumberland Avenue at 15th Street
Knoxville, TN 37996-4000
(423) 974-4480
www.lib.utk.edu/spcoll
www.lib.utk.edu/archives/
   hoskins.html

University of Texas at Arlington
Libraries, Special Collections Division
Box 19497
Arlington, TX 76019
(817) 272-3393
libraries.uta.edu/SpecColl/
   histmss.html

Tulane University
Manuscript Department
Jones Hall
New Orleans, LA 70118
(504) 865-5685
www.tulane.edu/~lmiller/
   Military.html

U.S. Army Military History Institute
22 Ashburn Drive
Carlisle Barracks
Carlisle, PA 17013-5008
(717) 245-3611
carlisle-www.army.mil/usamhi/

United States Military Academy
   Library
West Point, NY 10996
(914) 938-2954
usmalibrary.usma.edu

United States Naval Institute
   Library
118 Maryland Avenue
Annapolis, MD 21402
(410) 268-6110
www.usni.org

Virginia Military Institute Archives
Preston Library
Lexington, VA 24450
(540) 464-7566
web.vmi.edu/archives/

Virginia Tech
Carol M. Newman Library
Special Collections Department
Blacksburg, VA 24061
(540) 231-6308
spec.lib.vt.edu/civwar

Virginia War Museum
9285 Warwick Boulevard
Newport News, VA 23607
(757) 928-6738
www.warmuseum.org

Washington and Lee University
James Graham Leyburn Library
Special Collections
Lexington, VA 24450
(540) 463-8400
www.wlu.edu/~vstanley/
    speccoll.html

West Virginia University
WVU Libraries
West Virginia and Regional History
    Collection
P.O. Box 6464
Morgantown, WV 26506-6464
(304) 293-3536
www.libraries.wvu.edu/
    wvcollection/manuscripts/
    index.htm

Western Reserve Historical Society
10825 East Boulevard
Cleveland, OH 44106
(216) 721-5722
www.wrhs.org

University of Wisconsin–Milwaukee
Golda Meir Library, Archives
2311 East Hartford Avenue
Room W250
Milwaukee, WI 53201-0604
(414) 229-5402
www.uwm.edu/Library/arch/
    civilwar.htm

Wisconsin Veterans Museum
30 West Mifflin Street
Madison, WI 53703
(608) 267-1799
museum.dva.state.wi.us

Wright State University
Paul Laurence Dunbar Library
Special Collections and Archives
Dayton, OH 45435
(927) 775-2092
www.libraries.wright.edu/special/
    manuscripts/civwar.html

Suggested Books of Interest

Broadfoot, Thomas. *Civil War Books: A Priced Checklist With Advice.* 5th ed. Wilmington, NC: Broadfoot Publishing Co., 2000.

Cole, Harold L. *Civil War Eyewitnesses: An Annotated Bibliography of Books and Articles, 1955–1986.* Columbia, SC: University of South Carolina Press, 1988.

Dornbusch, Charles E. *Military Bibliography of the Civil War.* 3 vols. New York: New York Public Library, 1971–87; 4th vol., Dayton: Press of Morningside, 1987.

Dyer, Frederick H. *A Compendium of the War of the Rebellion.* 3 vols. New York: Thomas Yoseloff, 1959. Reprint. Dayton: Press of Morningside, 1994.

Evans, Clement A., ed. *Confederate Military History.* 18 vols. 1899. Reprint. Wilmington, NC: Broadfoot, 1987.

Fox, William F. *Regimental Losses in the American Civil War, 1861–1865.* 18th ed. Dayton: Morningside House, 1985.

Hall, Charles B. *Military Records of General Officers of the Confederate States of America.* Austin, TX: Steck Company, 1963.

Hewett, Janet B., et al. *Supplement to the Official Records of the Union and Confederate Armies.* 95 vols. Wilmington, NC: Broadfoot Publishing Co., 1994–99.

Lang, George, et al., comp. *Medal of Honor Recipients, 1863–1994.* 2 vols. New York: Facts on File, 1995.

Meredith, Lee W. *Guide to Civil War Periodicals.* 2 vols. Twentynine Palms, CA: Historical Indexes, 1991 and 1996.

Miller, Francis T., ed. *The Photographic History of the Civil War.* 10 vols. New York: Review of Reviews, 1912.

Murdock, Eugene C. *The Civil War in the North: A Selective Annotated Bibliography.* New York: Garland Publishing, 1987.

National Historical Society, *The Images of War: 1861–1865.* 6 vols. Garden City NY: Doubleday, 1982–84.

Nevins, Allan, et al. *Civil War Books: A Critical Bibliography.* 2 vols. Baton Rouge: Louisiana State University Press, 1967.

Quartermaster's Department. *Roll of Honor.* 27 vols. 1865–71. Reprint. Baltimore: Genealogical Publishing Company, 1994–96.

Sifakis, Stewart. *Compendium of the Confederate Armies.* 11 vols. New York: Facts on File, 1992–97.

Smith, Myron J., Jr. *American Civil War Navies: A Bibliography.* Metuchen, NJ: Scarecrow Press, Inc., 1992.

The Union Army. 8 vols. Madison, WI: Federal Publishing Company, 1908. Reprinted in 9 vols. Wilmington, NC: Broadfoot Publishing Company, 1998.

The Union Army: A History of Military Affairs in the Loyal States, 1861–65—Records of the Regiments in the Union Army—Cyclopedia of Battles—Memoirs of Commanders and Soldiers. 8 vols. Madison, WI: Federal Publishing, 1908.

United Confederate Veterans. *List of Organized Camps of the United Confederate Veterans.* New Orleans: Rogers' Printing Co., 1921.

U.S. Adjutant General's Office. *Official Army Register of the Volunteer Force of the United States Army, 1861–1865.* Washington, DC: Adjutant General's Office, 1865.

U.S. Naval War Records Office. *War of the Rebellion: A Compilation of the Official Records of the Union and Confederate Navies.* 30 vols. Washington, DC: Government Printing Office, 1874–1922.

U.S. Quartermaster's Department. *Roll of Honor, Names of Soldiers Who Died in Defense of the American Union, Interred in National Cemeteries, Numbers I–VI.* 1868. Reprint. Baltimore: Genealogical Publishing, 1994 (reprint of 1868).

U.S. War Department. *Atlas to Accompany the Official Records of the War of Rebellion.* Washington, DC: Government Printing Office, 1891–95.

U.S. War Department. *War of the Rebellion: A Compilation of the Official Records of the Union and Confederate Armies.* 128 vols. Washington, DC: Government Printing Office, 1880–1900.

Welcher, Frank J. *The Union Army, 1861–1865: Organizations and Operations.* 2 vols. Bloomington, IN: Indiana University Press, 1987–92.

The West Point Alumni Foundation. *Register of Graduates and Former Cadets of the United States Military Academy, 1802–1965.* Chicago: R. R. Donnelley & Sons, Co., 1965.

Wright, John. *Compendium of the Confederacy.* 2 vols. Wilmington, NC: Broadfoot Publishing Company, 1989.

About the Authors

Stephen McManus resides in Exton, Pennsylvania, with his wife, Berni, and their five children. A graduate of Rensselaer Polytechnic Institute and the Delaware Law School, he became interested in the Civil War as a school student, after learning that his great-great-great-grandfather, Stephen Thomas, had been an officer in the 18th Massachusetts infantry regiment.

Donald Thompson resides in Upper Marlboro, Maryland, with his wife, Linda. A graduate of Rhode Island College, he has a long-standing interest in the Civil War. As a child, he played with Civil War muskets that belonged to ancestors who served with the 18th Massachusetts Volunteer Infantry regiment. He is directly related to five men who served with the 18th Massachusetts, and also to Stephen Bucklin, a lieutenant colonel in the 3rd Rhode Island Heavy Artillery.

Thomas Churchill resides in Summerville, South Carolina, with his wife and three children. A graduate of The Citadel, the Military College of South Carolina, he traces his ancestry back to soldiers on both sides of the Civil War, including his great-great-grandfather, who was the color sergeant of the 18th Massachusetts. He finds it ironic that the college he attended and the place where he lives are in the heart of the area where so much Confederate history was made, yet he spends much of his time seeking information on a Union regiment from Massachusetts.